MONSTERS OF THE NORTHWOODS

**Paul and Robert Bartholomew,
William Brann, Bruce Hallenbeck**

North Country Books, Inc.
Utica, New York

Monsters of the Northwoods

Copyright © 1992
by
Paul and Robert Bartholomew,
William Brann, Bruce Hallenbeck

ISBN 0-925168-00-9

THIRD PRINTING 1992

Library of Congress Cataloging-in-Publication Data

Monsters of the Northwoods / by Paul & Bob
    Bartholomew, William Brann, Bruce Hallenbeck
    p.   cm.
    Includes bibliographical references.
    ISBN 0-925168-00-9
    1. Sasquatch—New York (State)   2. Sasquatch
    —Vermont.
I. Bartholomew, Paul, 1964-
QL89.2.S2M66   1992
001.9'44—dc20   92-23460
                                                                   CIP

Published by
North Country Books, Inc.
PUBLISHER—DISTRIBUTOR
18 Irving Place
Utica, New York 13501
315-735-4877

DEDICATION

*This book is dedicated with love and respect
to the late Dr. Warren L. Cook.
His unending quest and dedicated scientific
approach to the study of the unexplained will
be deeply missed. Also to Martha Hallenbeck
for courage and honesty in relating
her encounters with the unknown.*

ABOUT THE AUTHORS

Paul Bartholomew studied under Professor Warren Cook at Castleton State College in Vermont, where he has a degree in Communications and Journalism. He resides at R.F.D #2, Box 2886, Whitehall, New York 12887.

Robert Bartholomew is a radio reporter for WWSC in Glens Falls, New York.

William Brann is a member of the New York State Archaeological Association (Auringer Seelye Chapter), and engages in archaeology as an avocation. He has conducted over 400 separate excavations related to Native Americans. Mr. Brann has researched Bigfoot sightings in the northeast since the mid-1970's. He resides with his wife, Phyllis, at 2 Mountain View Drive, Hudson Falls, New York.

Bruce Hallenbeck is a former talk show host for WQBK in Albany, New York. A film critic who recently wrote and produced a full-length horror movie, *Vampyr*, Mr. Hallenbeck has published articles on a variety of subjects, including two volumes of poetry. He resides in Valatie, New York near Kinderhook.

ACKNOWLEDGMENTS

This book resulted from years of painstaking research and investigation. We thank the following witnesses: Royal Bennett, Shannon Rathbun, Susan Cook (for her patience), Al and Bob Davis, Herbert Francisco, Brian, Paul and Wilfred Gosselin, Fron Grabowski, Bart Kinne, Barry Knight, Mike Maab, Margaret Mayer, Martin Paddock, Cliff Sparks, Russell Zbierski, Joe Milo, Mike Eddy and others mentioned and anonymous. Researchers: Rick Barry, Walt Brundage, Archie Buckley, Bill Chapleau, Wes and Olga Gordeuk, Joseph Citro, Loren Coleman, Paul Cropper, Jameston Deveroux, Bob Girard, John Green, Zhou Guoxing, Tony Healy, Benton Jamison, Russ Kinne (for converting Bill's slides), Milton LaSalle, Dr. Gary Levine, Ron Lewis, Gary Mangiacopra, Lois O'Conners, Danny Perez, Ted and Jeff Pratt, Bob Rickard, Warren Thompson (for guidance), Dwight Whalen, Joe Zarzynski, Bill's original research team of Clifford South, Dick Newman, John King. Special people: Jim Caruso, Bob and Harry Diekel, Mary Dodge, Mark Dumas, Rob Dubois, Don Fangboner, John Gaelic, Bud Manell, Pauline Gosselin, Susan Hallenbeck, Dr. Grover Krantz, Bob Martell, Bill McLaughlin, Rusty Cook, Rolle Nedo, Terry O'Neil, Fred Palmer, Ray Parrott, and C. Prefountaine (with various members of the Whitehall School system), Karl Porter, Don Racette, Alan Taffel and PM Magazine crew, Roy Tracy (Bill's eyes and ears in the Adirondacks), George Van Guilder, Phil Winegard, Doug Williams (for locating maps). Special thanks to Emerson and Mary Bartholomew and family, Phyllis Brann and family, and the Hallenbeck family. We also thank various Whitehall Police Department members and several anonymous law officers. Reporters: Barney Fowler (*Albany Times Union*), George Greenough (*Whitehall Independent*), Tom Mitchell (*Rutland Herald*), Don Metivier (*Post Star*), Paul Rayno (*Moreau Sun*), Fred Styles (historical writer). Artists: Ed Congdon, Rob Dubois, Eric Miner.

TABLE OF CONTENTS

Foreword vi

Introduction vii

Chapter 1: The Historical Evidence 1

Chapter 2: The Lewiston Mystery 16

Chapter 3: The Abair Incident 22

Chapter 4: Beyond Abair 33

Chapter 5: The Kinderhook Creature 50

Chapter 6: The UFO Angle 78

Chapter 7: Vermont Encounters 84

Chapter 8: What Is It? 105

Summary 124

FOREWORD

That the Sasquatch, popularly known as "Bigfoot" roams the woods of New England will come as a surprise to most scientists as well as laymen. The evidence for the species' existence and ongoing reproduction—if not guaranteed survival—in this area of North America is impressive in its historical depth and for the numerous incidents in the 1970's and 1980's. The authors have approached this evidence with diligence and system, extracting the testimony as to when, where, who, and what was observed—setting the data forth often in the very words of the eyewitnesses, as gleaned from these dedicated investigators' taped interviews.

No one wants to be laughed at by their neighbors and it has been my experience that most sightings of hairy hominids in the northeastern U.S. go unreported in the media, and have to be ferreted out by investigators. Sasquatch research in New England is still bedeviled by much ignorance on the part of newspaper reporters, as well as scientists, who are not familiar with scholarly publications on this subject elsewhere in the nation, as well as in the Soviet Union and China, where the issue of relict hominid survival in the forests around us is taken more seriously. This volume, hopefully, will be a major step in the right direction—acquainting those open-minded enough to look at the evidence, so that the existence of this magnificent and fascinating species among us gets better known. Then, perhaps, when eyewitnesses have encounters, they will be less reluctant to come forth and tell us what they observed, so that those concerned with studying these highly intelligent beings can learn more about their patterns of behavior—not just to know, but to help these near-human creatures.

—*Warren L. Cook,* D.Litt., Ph.D.
Professor of History/Anthropology
Castleton State College

INTRODUCTION

It is a unique character of mankind to venture into the unknown. It also is characteristically human to cruelly ridicule those who do. Nothing tantalizes like the pursuit of some great mystery, but often the searcher's mission is a lonely one, which holds no guarantee of success. If the quest is one that is controversial, or as in this instance, challenges an established science, often the only public notice comes in the form of bitter skepticism, and questioning of the personal motivations and ethics of the seekers.

I have known one of the authors, Bill Brann, for many years, and have accompanied him on a few of his investigations. I have no doubts about his objectivity and integrity in the course of his examinations of evidence. I have seen many examples of his questioning approach to the information uncovered, and his determination to verify as much as possible each clue and testimonial. I regard this publication as the most dedicated effort by the authors to produce documentations of evidences, gathered from research spanning many years, which has been sifted and analyzed to the best of their abilities. The reader can find here a broad compilation of reports, some from unpublished personal testimony, published media, and evidences the researchers have found.

Canadian explorer Samuel de Champlain wrote an account of his first voyage to Canada in 1603 that was published in Paris. He told of believing the stories related to the Micmac Indians, who lived by the St. Lawrence River, about "un monstre 'epouvantable, that the natives called 'Gougou.'" It was described as a giant hairy beast that lived in the North American forests, and much feared by the Indians. French historian Marc Lescarbot publicly degraded Champlain's report of the stories. Writing in his *Historiere de la Nouvelle France*, in 1609, he used the example to cast a shadow of doubt on the veracity in all of Champlain's documentations. Champlain was the first to suffer public humiliation for reporting the legend of the North American creature of mystery. He would not be the last.

During the French and Indian War in 1759, a party of famous rangers led by Robert Rogers, legendary heroes depicted in the historical novel *Northwest Passage* by Kenneth Roberts, reported an encounter with such a giant upright hairy creature in northern Vermont. This monster was repeatedly seen, according to records of several of the northern Vermont townships, well into the 19th century.

There is nothing wrong with healthy skepticism. The authors of this publication will be the first to agree. But keep in mind that truth neither depends on belief, nor upon lack of it, and that truth often comes in the guise of the strange, the improbable, and sometimes, even the unbelievable.

—Paul Rayno
Former Historian
Washington County, New York

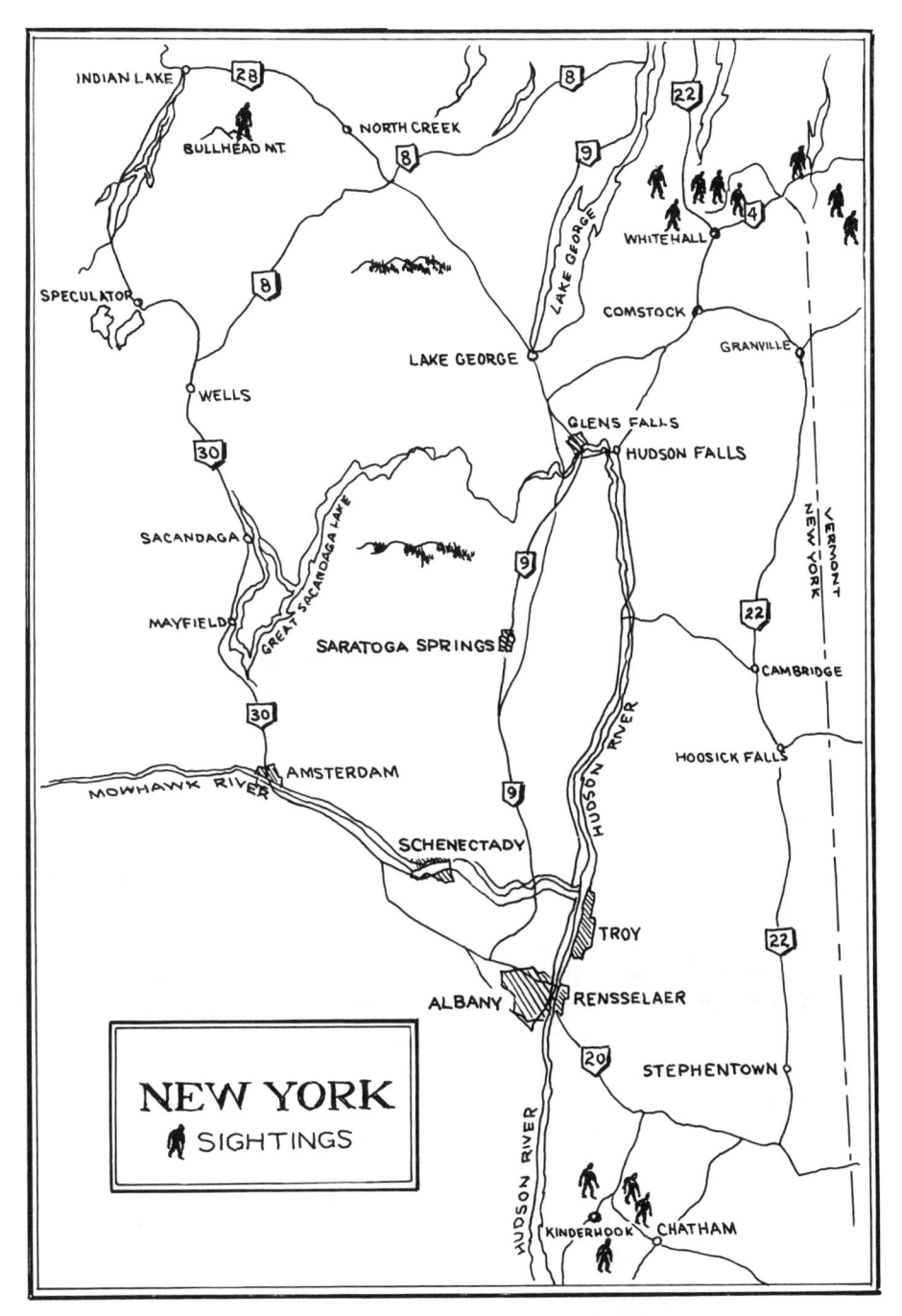

The authors have documented some one hundred forty sightings in New York State, some of which are shown on the above map.

Chapter 1

THE HISTORICAL EVIDENCE

All things are to be examined and called into question.
—Edith Hamilton

It sounds hard to believe that Bigfoot lurks in remote areas of New York and Vermont. Why aren't fossils, bodies or bones found? Where would it live? How would it elude capture? Yet how can you explain the numerous huge footprints that often track for miles in remote areas, the many close-up, multiple witness sightings by seemingly sane, upstanding citizens and law officers? Persistent reports within the same area have spanned over 380 years among the earliest European settlers. There are a number of apparently sincere, normal people who claim to have seen something that does not belong in the woods of New York and Vermont. No matter what the explanation we owe it to these people to examine the evidence from the earliest times to the present and objectively analyze the possibilities.

There are numerous references in historical literature to a hulking man-like creature inhabiting the remote mountains, thick woods and sparsely populated valleys of New York and Vermont. Legends of a man-beast are found in most North American Indian tribes, and the existence of such a "monster" has been intensely debated, even among the earliest settlers of the New World.

The Algonquin Indians were well acquainted with the Windigo, a "giant cannibalistic man" who did not wear clothes and had a hideous black mouth without lips. According to legend, its diet consisted of an unappetizing mixture of human flesh, rotten wood, mushrooms and swamp moss. He made sounds "like that which grouse make when they drum."[1] Even the bravest warrior feared the eerie hissing sounds and reverberating howls, noises frequently ascribed to modern-day Bigfoot.

The Iroquois maintained that the cannibalistic "Stone Giants" used rocks as weapons and with their powerful build, uprooted small trees.[2]

Indian legends of "wild men" or giant cannibals stretch across the border into Canada and Alaska, where the Eskimos called them "Tornit." In the Pacific Northwest, they were called "Sasquatch."[3]

In the upper St. Maurice River, in the Province of Quebec, the Algonquin-speaking Tete-de-Boule most commonly called this creature "Kokotshe." Other names included "Witiko" and "Atshen." Such tales of Stone Giants are interesting, but stories of huge man-like beings made of stone sound too far-fetched to bear any relationship to modern Bigfoot reports. Yet, on closer inspection it is clear that the legend does not discuss a creature made of stone but apparently one covered with fur or hair. According to John Cooper, writing in *Primitive Man*, the Tete-de-Boule legend states:

> He used to rub himself, like the animals, against the fir, spruce, and other resinous trees. When he was thus covered with gum or resin, he would go and roll in the sand, so that one would have thought that . . . he was made of stone.[4]

French explorer Samuel de Champlain presented the earliest account of such creatures in the region. During his first visit to America in 1603, while traveling along the St. Lawrence River of what is now Upstate New York, he wrote that scores of Indians recounted tales of a giant, hairy, human-like beast called "Gougou." Such stories were so numerous and widespread that Champlain himself believed them to be more than tales. Based on the sheer volume of reports from a variety of Indian tribes, he felt some type of "devil" surely existed in the region. Champlain wrote of the Micmac Indian legend he called "un monstre e'pouvantable."[5]

The explorer was so convinced of the beast's reality that he publicly affirmed its existence upon returning to France, beginning perhaps the first recorded Bigfoot or man-beast dispute. Like many modern-day witnesses, he was criticized by many, including noted French historian, Marc Lescarbot, author of *The History of New France*. Lescarbot publicly scorned Champlain for taking the Indian accounts seriously. It even cost him their friendship.

The following is the original English translation from French journal logs kept by Champlain during his exploration of the St. Lawrence in 1604:

> There is another strange thing worthy of narration, which many savages have assured me was true; this is, that near Chaleur Bay, towards the south, lies an island where makes his abode a dreadful monster, which the savages call Gougou. They told me it has the form of a woman, but most hideous . . . he has often devoured many savages. . . . This monster . . . makes horrible noises in that island, and when they speak of him it is with utterly strange terror, and many have assured me that they have seen him. Even . . . Sieur Prevert from St. Malo told me that, while going in search of mines . . . he passed so near the haunt of this frightful beast, that he and all those on board his vessel heard strange hissings from the noise it made, and that the savages he had with him told him it was the same creature, and were so afraid that they hid themselves wherever they could, for fear it should come to carry them off. And what makes me believe what they say, is the fact that all the savages in general fear it, and tell such strange stories of it, that if I were to record all they say, it would be considered untrue; but I hold that this is the dwelling-place of some devil that torments them in the manner described. This is what I have learned about this Gougou.[6]

In Champlain's narration, the Gougou's size is so large that "the tops of the masts of our vessels would not reach his waist. . . ." Although this sounds unbelievable, oral stories are often based on some truth. For example, there is a legend that contends if a young boy wants to become a fast runner, he must catch several butterflies and rub them on his body. Although rubbing the butterfly onto the skin has no effect on running ability, chasing such nimble creatures would enhance the boy's running strength and endurance.

While the French and Indian War raged during 1759, Major Robert Rogers and his band of rangers apparently encountered a Bigfoot-like creature while returning from an attack on the Indian village at St. Francis. The historical novel *Northwest Passage* by Kenneth Roberts, records the incident. According to the story, the group sailed from Crown Point up the northern-most tip of Lake Champlain at Missisquoi Bay, into what is now the Province of Quebec. A ranger scout named Duluth wrote of a strange encounter with a creature in northern Vermont, south of Missisquoi Bay, while a band of French and Indians attempting to avenge the attack, hotly pursued Duluth's group. He wrote that party members were persistenly annoyed "by a large black bear, who would throw large pine cones and nuts down upon us from trees and ledges; the Indians being disgusted" and naming him "wejuk or Wet Skine."

A decade later, the first settlers of northern Vermont heard tales of a suspiciously similar-looking creature bearing the related name, "Slippry Skin." The name can be found in numerous oral and written traditions throughout the state. No one knows whether a relationship exists between "Slippry Skin" and "Wet Skine," but descriptions of a similar creature in the region at about the same time period is conincidental indeed. Early historical records in Vermont abound with encounters of "Old Slippry Skin," which was said to resemble a huge bear. However, unlike any known bear, it mostly walked or ran upright on two legs. Bear-like encounters fill the histories of the townships of Morgan, Maidstone, Lemington and Victory. No doubt many reports have been embellished, but if even partially true, it would be difficult to believe that such a thing was an ordinary bear. They said it had a mean disposition and held grudges against humans.

According to Washington County, New York historian and Glens Falls *Post-Star* newspaper columnist, Paul Rayno:

> It ripped up fences and gardens, chased cows and sheep, dragged trees through cornfields and other crops, threw stones at school children and terrified hunters.
>
> It robbed smoke houses, pushed over haystacks, filled

sap buckets with stones, placed barbed wire into hayrakes and mowing machines, kicked over manure piles and dragged huge rocks into farm machinery which were almost impossible to remove.[7]

Reports referred to the creature's enormous size, with legs like "spruce logs." It didn't appear to be dangerous to humans but actually seemed to enjoy scaring people and farm animals.

So abundant were these "Slippry Skin" encounters that Vermont's Governor, Jonas Galusha, a well-known hunter, in a half-serious campaign gesture, ran for re-election by promising that he would personally bring in the beast. Paul Rayno commented on this somewhat exaggerated tale:

> His hunting party went into the woods where the beast had last been seen and set up camp. The governor, anointing himself with a liberal dose of 'scent of female bear,' went with his gun into the woods to stalk the creature. After a while the governor came charging into camp yelling 'Outta my way boys, I'm bringin' him back alive!" Slippryskin was tight on his heels. The entire party scattered, and no one thought to shoot at Slippryskin. The governor also lost the election.[8]

One party of hunters set out from the Town of Morgan, Vermont, to track down Slippry Skin, only to narrowly escape an ambush by the cunning superbear. As the story goes, the creature back-tracked on his old prints, rolling a huge tree down a mountainside. The group miraculously escaped, vowing never again to hunt the clever creature.

With Slippry Skin stories so abundant, it's curious no one ever shot this strange animal. To this day, no one knows what it was or where it went.

One of the earliest known newspaper accounts of a northeastern man-beast comes from Sackett's Harbor, New York, in 1818:

> Sackett's Harbor (N.Y.) Sept. 6
> ANOTHER WONDER
> Report says, that in the vicinity of Ellisburgh, was seen on the 30th Ult. by a gentleman of unquestionable

veracity, an animal resembling the Wild Man of the Woods. It is stated that he came from the woods within a few rods of this gentleman—that he stood and looked at him and then took his flight in a direction which gave a perfect view of him for some time. He is described as bending forward when running—hairy, and the heel of his foot narrow, spreading at the toes. Hundreds of persons have been in pursuit for several days, but nothing further is seen or heard of him.

The frequent and positive manner in which this story comes, induces us to believe it. We wish not to impeach the veracity of this highly favored gentleman—yet, it is proper that such naturally improbable accounts should be established by the mouth, of at least two direct eye-witnesses to entitle them to credit.[9]

Some twenty years later, in the summer of 1838, a young boy spotted a small black-haired wild man creature on the New York/Pennsylvania border. According to the Dorchester County, Maryland *Aurora* on August 27, 1838:

The . . . animal was seen in Silver Lake township about two weeks ago, by a boy some sixteen years old. We had the story from the father of the boy, in his absence, and afterward from the boy himself. The boy was sent to work in the backwoods near the New York State line. He took with him a gun, and was told by his father to shoot anything he might see, except persons or cattle.

After working for a while, he heard some person, a little brother he supposed, coming toward him whistling quite merrily. It came within a few rods of him and stopped.

He said it looked like a human being, covered with black hair, about the size of his brother, who was six or seven years old. His gun was some little distance off, and he was very much frightened. He, however, got his gun and shot at the animal, but trembled so that he could not hold it still.

The strange animal, just as his gun "went off," stopped behind a tree, and then ran off, whistling as before. The father said the boy came home very much frightened, and that a number of times during the afternoon, when thinking about the animal he had seen he would, to use the man's own words, 'burst out crying.'

Making due allowance for frights and consequent exaggeration, an animal of singular appearance has doubtless been seen. What it is, or whence it came, is of course yet a mystery.

Slippry Skin stories continued to be reported throughout the 1800's, with remarkably similar descriptions. The following story appeared on the front page of the *New York Times*, October 18, 1879:

A WILD MAN OF THE MOUNTAINS
Two Young Vermont Hunters Terribly Scared

Pownal, Vt., Oct. 17 — Much excitement prevailed among the sportsmen of this vicinity over the story that a wild man was seen on Friday last by two young men while hunting in the mountains south of Williamstown. The young men describe the creature as being about five feet high, resembling a man in form and movement, but covered all over with bright red hair, and having a long straggling beard, and with very wild eyes. When first seen the creature sprang from behind a rocky cliff, and started for the woods nearby, when, mistaking it for a bear or other wild animal, one of the men fired, and, it is thought, wounded it, for with fierce cries of pain and rage, it turned on its assailants driving them before it at high speed. They lost their guns and ammunition in their flight and dared not return for fear of encountering the strange being.

The newspaper continued to describe what appear to be "Old Slippry Skin" accounts:

There is an old story, told many years ago, of a strange animal frequently seen among the range of the Green Mountains resembling a man in appearance, but so wild that no one could approach it near enough to tell what it was or where it dwelt. From time to time, hunting parties, in the early days of the town, used to go out in pursuit of it, but of late years no trace of it has been seen, and this story told by the young men who claim to have seen it, revives again the old story of the wild man of the mountains. There is talk of making up a party to go in serach of the creature.

In autumn 1893, Long Islanders reported seeing a strange creature on several occasions in the vicinity of Rockaway Beach. According to the *New York Herald* of November 29, the "wild man" was first spotted about November 22 by "Red" McDowell and George Farrell while rowing one morning in desolate Rockaway Inlet, six miles south of Rockaway proper. Paddling towards shore for a closer look the creature uttered a series of "wild cries." The men quickly rowed off. The next evening John Louth saw a similar-looking being near some trees while driving through Rockaway Park. His 18-year-old daughter, Susie, was confronted by a creature the following day. She said it sprang from some bushes, knocked her down and ran off "uttering strange yells." It was described by witnesses as "a wild man, large in appearance, with fierce, bloodshot eyes, long, flowing, matted hair" and "shaggy" facial hair. There were numerous other sightings. Some believed the "beast" an insane sailor from the schooner *Maggie Devine* which ran ashore nearby weeks earlier with all hands saved but the first mate, James Rush, presumed drowned. Supporting this theory were witnesses who believed they could see a shoe on one foot of the figure and what may have been a tattered oilskin suit mistaken for a hide. The being also acted differently than most other sightings, occasionally attacking people. On the other hand, he or it, was never found and hunter "Ned" Tracy claimed to have come upon the creature eating a raw chicken. One might think even a delirious sailor would be able to find a more appetizing meal.

Two years later fantastic stories emerged from Delaware County, New York, in the small resort town of Margaretville, near Newburg.[10] The first incident was reported by Peter Thomas on the night of July 26. Driving a team of horses along a lonely road he was startled by the appearance of "a wild-eyed man or ape" which jumped out from underbrush and stood in the middle of the road "brandishing a pair of long and hairy arms and uttering a raucous, inarticulate cry." Thomas says he froze as it approached one of the horses, twisted its neck "with a faculty which betokened long practice" and dragged it off into the night. He was "too thoroughly frightened to give a definite description" other then being "seven feet high, of human shape, covered with hair." On July 27 farmer John Cook claimed to have been attacked and thrown by "a ferocious ape-like being" after shooting and apparently hitting it. Cook described the "wild man" as "about seven feet tall, entirely nude, covered with black hair, with a long beard and with teeth which project from his mouth like fangs." That same day a group of local boys and farmers hunting the creature found what they believed was its camp in the woods at nearby Rattlesnake Hill. A big fire was still smouldering and nearby were portions of the carcass of Mr. Thomas' horse, and scattered about were the bones and remains of cows, sheep and other animals.[11]

Curiously, the bones had been split and the marrow eaten out.

Long Island was a hotbed of ape-like creature sightings during the early decades of the 20th century. In February 1909 residents of the Long Island communities of Patchogue, Eastport, Quogue and Westhampton reported seeing on numerous occasions a strange creature that emitted a "blood-curdling shriek."[12] Although no one ever had a really good look at the nocturnal mystery beast that frequented the woods, it was said to "glare out of the thickets with eyes of flame." As we shall later see, fiery red glowing eyes that apparently self-illuminate are common in Bigfoot reports.

Several of those who had glimpsed the creature, described it as a "baboon" or "monkey-like." Many residents of Westhampton supported the baboon theory and corroborated it with their own sightings. In "Robinson Crusoe" fashion, the residents said it was "to have come ashore on the wreckage of a deep bark" the previous fall "and to have taken to the woods." Several attempts to hunt down the creature were unsuccessful. According to the *New York Herald* of February 7, 1909, "Strong men with guns [went] into the forests at dead of night to find the thing, be it bird or devil, panther or baboon." Nothing was ever found.

Thirteen years later in early November 1922, reports circulated of the existence of a "ferocious baboon in the wilds of Long Island," near Babylon. Residents became frightened, and, by November 5th, the situation escalated to such a feverish pitch that search parties with armed hunters began scouring the woods. Creature reports varied, with descriptions ranging from a "baboon" to a "gorilla."[13]

In 1931, there were more reports of a "wandering gorilla or perhaps a chimpanzee" in the Huntington area.[14] The "ape-like . . . hairy creature—about four feet tall" was spotted on several occasions. It was first reported during June near Mineola, Long Island, when six people at Lewis and Valentine's nursery were frightened by the creature. Police, armed with weapons, found no trace after an extensive search. A check by the Nassau County Police Department of zoos in the region found that no animals were missing. By June 29 the 'hysteria' had spread, building to such a point that Captain Earl Comstock directed about a dozen armed police units in organized search parties. About two dozen local volunteers assisted. They found nothing, with the exception of some curious tracks which seemed to be solely those of the hind feet, about the size of a man's hand, though the thumb was set further back than would be the case with a human.

During July, the thing appeared throughout the Huntington area. On the 18th, a nurseryman and his family told authorities they saw a gorilla-like creature crashing through a portion of shrubbery. A farmer reported seeing a similar-looking "strange animal" about three miles from the site. In both cases, police found tracks, only to lose them in the nearby woods. Not far away is Mount Misery, where mystery writer and journalist John Keel has recorded many sightings of a man-like monster. And, in Amityville, later to be the site of a famous haunting, an "eight-foot-tall gorilla with glowing red eyes" was reported on several occasions during the early 1930s. The Amityville scare may have no relationship at all with Bigfoot reports in the area several decades later, but the coincidence is thought-provoking.

It was 6:35 p.m., November 13, 1974, when Suffolk County Police responded to a call at 112 Ocean Avenue in Amityville, Long Island. Police found six bullet-ridden bodies. Twenty-four-year-old Ronald DeFeo was later convicted for killing his family with a high-powered rifle as they slept. DeFeo mercilessly pumped bullets into the bodies of his two brothers and sisters, and both parents. While confessing, he said, "It just started; it went so fast, I just couldn't stop."

DeFeo later testified during the trial that for several months leading up to the shooting, "I heard voices. Whenever I looked around, there was no one there, so it must have been God talking to me." The next year, on December 18, 1975, the Lutz family moved into the house and were the subject of the now famous book, "The Amityville Horror."[15]

Let's step back in time forty years. Amityville was the site of a "Beast" or "Demon" mysteriously roaming through neighborhoods at night. The following story appeared in the *New York Herald Tribune*, September 5, 1934:

MAN, BEAST OR DEMON? IT'S LOOSE IN AMITYVILLE

Mysterious Apelike Marauder
Raids Garage; Town on Guard
Special to the Herald Tribune

Amityville, L.I., Sept. 4—

The mysterious animal, described by some as a large monkey, which was first seen in this section last week, paid a visit early this morning to the home of Mrs. Alfred C. Abernathy, of Bennett Place, South Amityville, tore up an old fur coat, ripped several mattresses and clawed an old automobile in the garage. Tonight most of the male residents of the neighborhood are sitting on their porches waiting for the animal with shotguns, rifles, revolvers and garden hoses.

No one has solved the mystery of whatever it was, be it beast or demon, roaming the vicinity of Amityville, Long Island, during the mid-1930s. Is there a link between these reports and the hauntings? For those unacquainted with Bigfoot-lore it would be easy to conclude that the answer is no, but some researchers actually believe that there is a connection between reports of Bigfoot-type creatures and so-called psychic or paranormal phenomena. Some fundamentalists actually contend that Bigfoot is a demonic creature referred to in the Bible, which will appear during the last days of the world. We will briefly examine both of these admittedly far-out sounding theories in Chapter 8.

The early 1930s also saw a wild beast scare to the north in the rustic Adirondack Mountains.

No one knows for certain, but the first creature to have been called "Bigfoot" was likely an ordinary man retreating back to nature in the deep-forested Adirondack Mountains to live off the land. The "creature," as he was called, was sighted several times and was often described as being an enormous, hairy "wild man" with a footprint "nearly a yard across."

Residents forgot about the tale until a rash of Bigfoot reports in Whitehall, New York during 1976 brought retired Sergeant Walter E. Dixon, stationed for years with Troop B of the New York State Police, to relate the yarn of the Adirondack "wild man." The actual story was recorded by Glens Falls *Post-Star* newspaper reporter Donald Metivier.

The wild man had been blamed for burning down several lumber camps and cabins in the Hamilton County area, north of Lake George. State Police finally made an effort to capture the man on a cold night in February 1932. Two cousins, Dick Farrell and Reg Spring of Indian Lake were trapping roughly two miles south of Blue Mountain Lake. The two trappers found an abandoned cabin near O'Neil Flow and began heading toward the loft for some sleep when they saw what appeared to be a large creature peering in the window. It seemed to be covered from head to foot with hair and, as it ran away, it left deep footprints in the snow.

The two cousins, understandably frightened, travelled to Indian Lake and contacted Farrell's brother, Jack, a conservation officer. He organized a search party that went into the O'Neil Flow area after the "wild man." Lt. Charles B. McCann of Troop B State Police led the posse. In the party were Ernest Blanchard and Charles Turner of Indian Lake, Trooper Addison Hall, the Farrell brothers, and Spring. When they reached the cabin, they tracked the footprints of the "creature"; the tracks were thirty inches long, very wide and easy to follow in the snow.

On the second day of their search, they supposedly found a cabin in an old lumber camp near Dunbrook Mountain in the chain lakes area of the town of Newcomb. The men quickly surrounded the camp. They beckoned to the "creature" to surrender. Apparently, though, it jumped out a window and dashed off in the snow. It crouched by a pile of logs and reportedly said: "I just want to be left alone. Go away." As the posse advanced closer, the "creature" (which by now everyone realized was a man) fired a shotgun blast, felling Turner in the snow. Lt McCann ordered the men to return the fire, and a barrage of lead brought the man down. Cautiously, the group inched forward and realized that they had killed the famed "wild man." Removing several layers of untanned deer and bear skins from his body and found that he was in fact, a 5-foot, 6-inch, 160-pound black man. The mystery of the Adirondack "wild man" was solved.

Although Turner was struck in the hip, the wound wasn't serious. The men returned to town, where they brought Hamilton County Coroner Dr. H. F. Carroll, who walked more than ten miles on snowshoes to reach the body, which was subsequently brought to Burt Swain's Funeral Parlor in North Creek on a toboggan. The identity of the wild man remains a mystery. In addition to the burned shotgun in his possession, he was carrying four dollars in Canadian currency. Hamilton County authorities wouldn't spend public funds to bury him, refusing to pay $75 dollars to put the mystery man to rest. It is believed he was eventually buried in Potters Field at North Creek in an unmarked grave in the corner of the cemetery.

How had the wild man made such large footprints? Police discovered that he wrapped his feet in layers of bearskins making a huge snowshoe that enabled him to scurry over the snow without sinking too deeply, leaving behind the large prints. According to those involved, the name "Bigfoot" was coined to describe the yard-long tracks of the unfortunate wild man.

It's a colorful story, and those involved swore the truth of every word. But whether or not the origin of the term "Bigfoot" can be traced to the Adirondack region, there is no doubt that a rich tradition of such creatures—not men, but something quite different—has existed since the White Man's arrival.

References:

1. Guinard, Joseph E., "Witiko Among the Tete-de-Boule," in *Primitive Man*, Volume 3, 1930, pp. 69-70. Also, Rapp, Marvin A., "Legend of the Stone Giants," *New York Folklore Quarterly*, Winter, 1956, Volume 12, Number 4. Clark, Jerome and Coleman, Loren, *Creatures of the Outer Edge*. New York: Warner, 1978.
2. Ibid.
3. Clark, Jerome and Coleman, Loren, *Creatures of the Outer Edge*. New York: Warner, 1978, pp. 58-59.
4. Cooper, John M., Catholic University of America, writing in *Primitive Man*, Volume 6, "The Cree Witiko Psychosis," pp. 20-24.
5. Rayno, Paul, "Pioneers and Patriots," March 26, 1975, p. 10, in the Glens Falls, NY *Post-Star*. Column article entitled, "He Lost Old Slippryskin—and Election." Also, a series of four columns by Rayno, in the *Post-Star*. "Human-Like Hairy Beasts," appearing late August 1977; "More Hairy Beasts," September 7, 1977; "A Vicious Beast," September 14, 1977; and "Lingering Questions," September 21, 1977. Also, taped interview with Rayno by Bill Brann, 1977.
6. This quotation is an English translation from the logs of Samuel de Champlain of the experiences recorded while exploring the St. Lawrence Valley in 1604. It appeared in Volume 1 of a 6-volume work entitled, *"The Works of Samuel de Champlain, reprinted, translated and annotated by six Canadian scholars under the general editorship of H.P. Biggar*. Volume 1 covers 1599-1607, translated and edited by H.H. Langton and W.F. Ganong, with the French texts collated by J. Home Cameron. Reprinted by the University of Toronto Press, 1971. The narration appears on pages 187-188 in Chapter XII, titled, 'Of a frightful monster which the savages call Gougou, and of our short and favourable passage back to France.'
7. Rayno, Paul, "Pioneers and Patriots," March 26, 1975, p. 10, in the Glens Falls, NY *Post-Star*. Article entitled, "He Lost Old Slippryskin—and Election.,"
8. Ibid.
9. *Exeter Watchman*, September 22, 1818.
10. *Newburg Daily Press* (New York), July 29, 1895, "Delaware County's Wild Man." Also, *The New York Herald*, July 31, 1895, "He, She or It—Beast or Human. Wild Thing Loose in Delaware County and Scaring the Natives Half Silly." I am indebted to Gary Mangiacopra of 7 Arlmont Street, Milford, CT for locating both articles. In *The Bigfoot Casebook* by Janet and Colin Bord (Stackpole 1982), this incident is incorrectly reported to have occurred in "Delamere" County, NY.
11. *Newburg Daily Press* (New York), July 29, 1895.
12. "Shrieking Apparition Rouses Long Island: Wild, Weird Cries Disturb the Thickets in the Neighborhood of Quogue, and Armed Men, All in Vain, Seek the Lair of the Mysterious Thing." *New York Herald*, February 7, 1902, Section 2, p. 7.

13. *Washington Post* (Washington, DC), November 6, 1922, p. 1, "Seek Ferocious Baboon in Wilds of Long Island."

14. Keel, John A., *Strange Creatures from Time and Space*. Greenwich, CT: Fawcett, 1970, pp. 95-96.

15. Ansen, Jay, *The Amityville Horror*. New York: Bantam, September 1977, in arrangement with Prentice-Hall. Aronson, Harvey, and Sullivan, Gerard, *The Amitville Murders*. New York: Coward, McCann & Geoghegan, 1981.

Chapter 2

THE LEWISTON MYSTERY: BIGFOOT BEAR OR MUTANT?

Since about 1960, scores of residents in the vicinity of Lewiston, nestled in the northwestern corner of New York State, claim to have seen a Bigfoot-type creature in the woods and open fields of the region. It is a small close-knit community on the Canadian border just north of Niagara Falls. The animal is typically described as covered with black hair or fur and is a bit more stout than relatives in other sections of the state.

Peter Filicetti, a part-time village police officer takes the reports seriously, having personally interviewed over fifty people claiming to have either seen or heard it. A composite of the creature has it standing "between 5 feet 6 inches and 6 feet tall . . . [and] between 300 and 350 pounds." Filicetti first became interested in the creature after it apparently took an interest in him. He was with his mother, picking sweet corn on his parents' farm in September 1976, when something strange happened. He told a staff writer for the *Niagara Falls Review*, Linda Powless, "We were picking corn when I looked up and saw rows of corn separating."[1] This was followed by a grunting noise and what sounded like something very large running. Mustering courage to investigate, Officer Filicetti described what he found as "unbelieveable"—rows of trampled corn and a trail of prints extending over 200 yards, which he later lost in a marshy area. "They were footprints, not paw prints!" he emphasized. There was one other unusual aspect to the tracks; they had only three toes. Alarmed, to say the least, he banded together nine friends and some dogs, and ventured out on a search party determined to track down whatever it was. The creature left them scratching their heads, however. "We came up empty-handed . . . even with the dogs we couldn't find a trace of it," he said.[2]

Several months later he was working in his parents' garage at the farm late into the night when he got an overwhelming feeling of being watched. It bothered him so he finally covered up the windows. From then on, the Lewiston Bigfoot was more than a passing interest.

In September 1978, Officer Filicetti received a spectacular phone call from two fire-fighting buddies. It would turn out to be one of the most controversial incidents in the history of the Lewiston Bigfoot. Could he come down to the firehouse, they asked? Hunters, they explained, had come across the carcass of what appeared to have been a dead Bigfoot. Kevin Mooradian and David Holt were hunting pheasant in the vicinity of Lutts Road in the nearby Town of Porter, when they stumbled across the find in a field by an abandoned labor camp once used for migrant workers. Filicetti grabbed his camera and raced to the fire station. Lying on the floor were the severed head and feet "that were nothing like I had ever seen before," he later remarked. His first reaction was disbelief and skepticism. The ape-like head had two ferocious-looking four to six-inch fangs resembling something from a horror movie. "I yanked on the tusks to see if they had been planted there. They didn't budge. I checked inside the mouth to see if there were any incisions to show that they had been sewn in. There weren't." He said, "I kicked it, turned the head and feet over. It was real." Filicetti started snapping away with his camera. The feet had five human-appearing toes.

But, as so frequently happens in such spectacular cases, the evidence was lost, making absolute scientific identification impossible. "I could kick myself for not impounding it right then and there," the frustrated officer said. According to Filicetti, one of the hunters kept possession of the remains in a backyard trash bag. "Dogs apparently pulled the bag apart and the hunter's next door neighbor found the head on his front lawn and threw it in his backyard," he said. That was the last anyone ever saw of the head.

The hunters' careless actions seem out of character for people who supposedly believed the remains may have been that of Bigfoot, as, if proven true, they would have been instant celebrities; the only people in the history of man to have made such a discovery—the find of the century if not of the millennium. Yet, the explanation as to how the remains were lost sounds reasonable enough. While still at the firehouse, one of the hunters told Filicetti that he'd like to keep the remains, let the head decay and use it for a mantelpiece. That's why the hunter had reportedly left it in the yard. After realizing his mistake, Filicetti pulled out all the stops to locate the head, but to no avail. "We even pulled in a bloodhound from the sheriff's department to locate the head but couldn't find it. Dogs must have dragged it off somewhere," the disappointed officer concluded.

The mystery of the Bigfoot head caused a stir for several months, with local residents being fairly split in opinions. The tabloids had a field day. The *Weekly World News* of April 29, 1980, splashed the case across the front page in bold headlines which proclaimed: "NEWS EXCLUSIVE . . . BIGFOOT PHOTOS BAFFLE EXPERTS . . . Family of bizarre creatures may be roaming the wilds."[3] Although the location of the skull is still a mystery, and no physical evidence remains, there appears to be little doubt as to what the object was in the picture. Responding to a letter from Paul Bartholomew to Dr. Sidney Anderson, Department of Mammalogy, American Museum of Natural History in New York City, the animal expert wrote:

> What I saw was the photograph of the severed head of a black bear . . . Nothing strange about that.[4]

Paul also contacted Richard W. Thorington, Jr., Curator of Mammals, National Museum of Natural History, Smithsonian Institution. He stated, "I looked at the photos you mentioned in your letter of 24 April. I think the animal was a black bear."[5]

Although the mystery of the "Bigfoot skull" was apparently solved, sightings continue. One theory receiving prominent attention among Lewiston residents is the possibility the reports may be of a bear mutated by chemicals. The vicinity of Lewiston harbors several toxic dumpsites. Lewiston Town

Clerk, Mary Beth Brado, expressed the fear of many residents who give credence to the mutant hypothesis. She mentions possible emissions from a container filled with radioactive materials several decades ago which may have resulted in a new form of life.[6] Dr. Stuart Scott, Assistant Professor of Archeology, State University of New York at Buffalo, shoots down the atomic waste theory, however. Scott notes that no such creatures have been reported in the vicinity of Hiroshima and Nagasaki since the atom bomb was dropped in August, 1945.[7]

One newspaper columnist who took a skeptical view was Joseph Ognibene, writing in the *Niagara Gazette*, March 9, 1980:

> ABOUT BIG FOOT. By now I am sure you have all heard about the creature that is supposed to be down around the Lewiston-Youngstown area. I heard about it months ago and checked it out.
>
> The carcass . . . photographed was the remains of a bear, I was told. It had been discarded by a hunter, which in itself is disgusting. If a fellow is going to take a bear he should eat it, have a mount made or make a rug from the hide.
>
> Back to Big Foot. The carcass was hauled around by neighborhood dogs until it was mauled and stretched out of shape. By the time it was spotted the skin had deteriorated and was shrinking from the skull. The skin pulled and caused the canine teeth of the bear to protrude making them look like tusks.
>
> I have refused before to give credence to such nonsense, but have had so many fellows and gals ask about it, I had to mention it today. Can you imagine a creature that would choose to live in the Lewiston-Youngstown area with all those people, cars and chemical dumps when it could wander toward the Adirondacks and live in peace? Big Foot sightings are like flying saucer sightings. Everyone knows someone who knows someone else whose cousin's wife's friend saw one. As soon as the Big Foot flap has run its course, maybe we can go back to something sensible, like the panther sightings of a few years ago.[8]

But some residents remained firmly unconvinced. Partly because a popular spot for the creatures to be sighted is a government reserve area where atomic waste was dumped during World War II. Filicetti says, "Some people believe these creatures are bears that drank or ate something contaminated with nuclear waste or radiation."

There have been a number of reports emanating from the nearby Tuscarora Indian Reservation. Not all Indians are believers, but Chief Frank Wasko is. After hearing several stories about a strange creature he feels, "Something is out there, we just don't know what it is. We've heard about it for years"[9] Wasko believes an atomic silo at the reserve base may have leaked resulting in mutated bears.

The Lewiston area is dotted with dozens of caves and thick forested woodlands that could possibly harbor some type of strange creature. As Linda Powless of the *Niagara Falls Review* writes, "Hoax or real, something is frightening the residents of Lewiston." What that "something" is, be it human nature or an unknown creature, remains a mystery.

References:

1. Powless, Linda, "The Lewiston Bigfoot: A Big Hoax or A Mutant? Scary creatures terrorize Lewiston residents," *Niagara Falls Review*, Monday, March 17, 1980, p. 4.
2. Billington, Michael, "Bigfoot? Shadowy Creature Keeps to Dark Places in Lewiston," *Buffalo Courier-Express*, March 3, 1980, p. 4.
3. *Weekly World News*, April 29, 1980, pp. 1, 19.
4. Letter from Dr. Sidney Anderson, American Museum of Natural History, Central Park West at 79th St., New York, NY 10024, dated May 26, 1980, to Paul Bartholomew.
5. Letter from Richard W. Thorington, Curator of Mammals, National Museum of Natural History, Smithsonian Institution, Washington, DC, dated April 30, 1980, to Paul Bartholomew.
6. Taddeo, Lily, "UB Profs Still Skeptical About 'Big Foot,'" *Lockport Union-Sun*, March 3, 1980.
7. Ibid.

8. Ognibene, Joseph, "Forget that 'Bigfoot,'" article appearing in the "Outdoor Scene" column of *Niagara Gazette*, March 9, 1980.

9. Powless, Linda, "The Lewiston Bigfoot: A Big Hoax Or A Mutant? Scary creatures terrorize Lewiston residents," *Niagara Falls Review*, Monday, March 17, 1980, p. 4.

Chapter 3

THE ABAIR INCIDENT

On August 24, 1976, Paul Gosselin and Martin Paddock witnessed a strange creature in a field near Abair Road, rural Whitehall, New York. Paul was a good looking boy of 18, easy-going and very cooperative. We sat in my car for the better part of an hour as he began telling his story. Somewhere off in the distance a machine buzzed annoyingly. Yet, I found myself hopelessly involved with his story. We then drove to an area not far from Gosselin's home and stopped beside a farm on Abair Road. Paul began pointing out where they first heard and saw the creature. I didn't think it would be difficult to prove a man-like creature such as Bigfoot had taken up residence in the Whitehall area; I was mistaken. For fifteen years I have hunted and researched this small upstate community near the Vermont State line.

Lighting a cigarette, Paul began: "It was about 10 p.m. when Marty Paddock and I saw a large human form standing on the side of the road. We went down to the end of the road, turned around and came back. We stopped and heard a sound like a pig squealing or a lady screaming. We drove off to the top of the hill, locked the doors on the truck, I loaded the gun and pointed it out the window. We turned around and drove to the opposite side of the road so I could have a better shot at it."

The two men sat there staring into the darkness. Suddenly, Paul saw the creature standing not far from a telephone pole located about 70 feet from the shoulder of the road. He said it began running toward the truck. "I couldn't speak. Finally I blurted out, 'Marty, get the hell out of here!'" Paddock's green pickup responded, leaving 57 feet of rubber etched into the macadam. It momentarily fish-tailed down the road.

"We went back to town and told the cops, and no one would believe us.[1] Then we picked up a friend, Bart Kinney." The threesome returned to Abair Road.

Gosselin continues: "I knew just what it was as soon as I saw it. It scared me—it scared me a lot. What really attracted me was the eyes on it; big red eyes. It just stood there. It didn't move or nothing. It was seven to eight feet tall, about 300-400 pounds and it had thick, short, brown, coarse hair. On its head, longer hair. We returned and reported it to the Whitehall Police who notified Whitehall State Police and the Sheriff's Patrol. There were eleven of us all together. Eight were police officers."

Paul's father was an off-duty police sergeant in Whitehall who joined the group. Paul tells how he and his father walked into the field and heard a powerful scream. "We were kneeling down listening and watching when it screamed. We got up and walked back to the roadside."

We were in the left-hand side of the field on Abair Road. Down in the right-hand side of the field there is a fence-line. "A sheriff shined a spotlight up there and saw something walking along the fence. He yelled out, 'What the hell was that?' He backed his car up, keeping it in the light. I knew just what it was as soon as he shined the light on it. He got a perfect look at it, but later he wouldn't admit it, afraid everyone would make fun of him. The remains of a deer were found within the field."

There were some residents who claimed what the boys saw that night was an escaped gorilla. I asked Paul about this, and he claimed what he saw walked straight up like a man. He emphasized very clearly it was *no gorilla*. By this time witnesses were getting a little gun-shy of all the news media coverage. Paddock agreed to talk to me. I found him working at a corner service station in Whitehall: "It was standing on a knoll not far from the shoulder of the road. I really didn't get a real good look at it then, but seeing it later, I would describe it as being seven to eight-foot tall, weighing more than 300 pounds. It was muscular, big and stocky. The eyes were not red, like glowing; I think they just reflected the red in the lights. All I know is it was something big and we got out of there in a hurry."

Bart Kinney, the third member of the trio, stated: "It was in the field 500 to 600 feet away. I never saw the face. It was about seven to eight feet tall and stooped from the shoulders as it walked. The creature was moving rather slow when I saw it. It was no bear, I know that. A bear doesn't walk like that."

Off-duty police sergeant Wilfred Gosselin said he waited for over an hour but didn't see the creature again.

Paul's older brother, Brian, a member of the Whitehall Police Department, who called the State Police and Sheriff's Patrol to check out the story the following night, had his own encounter while off duty. "Myself and one of the state troopers were out there and I was turning around in the middle of the road and he was down the far end turning around. My headlights on the car picked up a pair of eyeballs. Big, red eyeballs, and I turned the lights of the car off. I shined my flashlight out there and that's when I [saw] the thing look right at me."

"I called the trooper on the C.B. He went up into the field where the creature had been seen and spotlighted the hedgerow. I turned off the lights and engine and waited in the dark. Something came crashing through the woods. I turned my headlights back on and the creature was about thirty feet in front of me. I stepped out of the car; the window was down on the driver's side." Gosselin knelt in a firing position, his arm fully extended through the window, his .357 service revolver cocked and ready to fire.

When asked why he didn't fire, he responded, "It was very human-like. You would have had to have been there to understand; then I could ask you the same question. All it did was stand there. It put its hands in front of its eyes. Hands? I don't know if that's what they were. I couldn't see any fingers. All it did was scream at the top of his lungs. I watched him for a good minute. Then he turned around and started back into the woods. It went about 7½ to 8 feet tall and weighed about 400 pounds. . . ."

"It had big, red eyeballs that bulged about a half-inch off his face. As far as the mouth and nose, I didn't notice any. I was too scared and too shook up. As far as ears go, I saw none. It had no tail and it doesn't walk on all fours, it walks on two, like a man would. It's covered with hair, dark brown, almost black and the back end of it, the hair was more or less wore off because you can see the cheeks of the buttocks sticking out through the hair that was more or less worn. He was covered with clay on the backside. His arms hung just about eight to ten inches below his knees. He walks with a hunch and it didn't run, although it could move fast."

The next morning Brian Gosselin and his brother returned to the field. The tracks that were found in the matted grass were more than twice as large as a man's and had a five-foot stride. The two men later found a large impression along the stream bed flowing into the Poultney River from the New York State side, just down from Carver's Falls, New York. Two years before the sighting, a hunter near Abair Road reported seeing something in the woods that frightened him so badly he refused to hunt the area again.

Within about a mile of Abair Road a few nights after the original sightings, a school teacher encountered a large seven to eight-foot tall creature that crossed the road directly in front of her car near an apple orchard. A quantity of partially eaten apples were found. There were also indications that something large and heavy walked through the area, but nothing in the way of toes could be distinguished. The orchard owner's dogs were barking and whining throughout the night.

Nights later, following the Abair Road incidents, a deputy sheriff (wishing anonymity) on patrol saw a large figure in the field. His description goes as follows: "I didn't have any binoculars with me so I was unable to see the face. It was seventy-five to one hundred yards away, moving along a hedgerow. I stand five feet, eight inches, and I could barely see over the hedgerow . . . and his shoulders and arms were above it. It swung its arms with a stride. I put the spotlight on it. It was no bear, of that I'm sure. It walked the length of the hedgerow which is forty to fifty yards long. I just can't explain it."

"It had long arms and it was furry. I watched it cut down across Abair Road and through the pines down along Waite Road. I wouldn't say it walked with a five-foot stride from the impressions I saw in the meadow. The only comparison I can make is I have this big sergeant and he's well over six feet, weighs about 300 pounds. He wears a size 56 jacket. He has to stoop down when he comes through a doorway. The thing I [saw] was bigger than him."

The deputy's interest in the creature pursued him even when off duty. "My wife, two other family members and myself, on September 7, journeyed to some of the most remote areas along the Poultney River in hopes of getting a look at the creature or at least, find footprints. Everything's been flooded and all the sediment sand is scattered along the intervals and all along the river banks, making it ideal to find prints. It's that fine silt and sand and it dried hard. I found my tracks right on the Poultney River between Gould Road and Abair Road where the bridge comes across from Vermont. I went along the river bank. That's where we found the tracks and the one good print."

"It looks to me like he [came] up from the river . . . stepped on a moss-covered log and you can see where the foot slid off, leaving a large impression. It's heavy, and where I could walk along the bank where it had given way, I found a heel mark. That impression was about six inches deep. The sediment was wet there. We'd had several days of recent rain. There was about 2½ inches of sand that washed off the bank and obliterated some of the tracks. There was a rivulet right right along next to one of the prints. The three prints that I have measured looked like it was made by the same one. The cast that I made off one of the better prints measures 19½ inches long from big toe to heel, 8½ inches across the toes; across the arch is 5¼ inches, at the heel 4¼. . . . When I walked on it in a normal walk, I hardly sunk or bruised the sand, and I weigh 220 pounds. The impressions I found were pressed a good half-inch into the sediment deposit."

"What I believe to be a nesting area sets right on the interval. Brush was deposited there from the flooding earlier in the spring. The brush was treaded down in the center like something large had bedded there. There were chunks of bark laid on the ground covering the wet sand under an old tree. It had to be something large that had done it, and intelligent. There was corn pulled up and stalks were carried to the area. There were four piles of stool, more than a human could do . . . no fur in it but there was corn. I didn't think to take a sample. The type of corn found there was interval. It looked like it could have been its basic diet. Earlier that day we heard vocalizations off in the distance. It was some weird scream. It's no animal I've ever heard, and I've hunted here since I was a boy. It sounded as though it was giving a warning. The way I'd describe it is a high-pitched squeal or shrill scream. . . . I think we disturbed it. I don't know if it saw or sensed us. The vocalizations seemed to be moving off in the distance. A friend of mine had a similar experience. He heard high-pitched squeals . . . something really excited and enraged while he was hunting the area the fall before. He never saw what made the sound and never found a track. Whatever it was, stayed in the area."

"There was a mounted patrol that searched another location from where I was. The deputies searched the marsh. They buried their horses right up to their stomachs. The animals acted spooked. They checked the caves. There was no evidence that it had ever used them. I took the cast that I had made to show a fellow officer that was with the mounted patrol. He owns an attack dog that would normally come to me. I was holding the cast. The animal just bristled up, snarled and backed away. I figured he picked up scent from it. I remember how the boys that first saw the creature were ridiculed. I thought when I made the cast, that type of criticism would have stopped. It didn't, and I became ridiculed myself. The deputy's wife then spoke up. 'My husband has taken a lot of ribbing, but I [saw] the tracks. Let them explain to us what made them.'"

The cast was borrowed for study for two weeks. It was returned without a written report on the findings. The deputy continued: "A carcass of a 125-pound deer was found torn apart in a field off Abair Road. . . . One lady lost a colt and some goats. I don't think it has anything to do with what we were talking about."

"There's an elderly gentleman that lives in one of the most rural areas in these parts. I was told that he had at least two sightings of the creature over the years. The area's all ledges; there's land back in there that possibly has never been hunted. He won't confirm his sightings in fear people will think he's crazy or senile. I know he's a very gentle man who believes in live and let live. It's not bothering him so why should he bother it."

The incidents along Abair Road affected Paul and Brian Gosselin in the form of sleepless nights and recurring nightmares for several months. Police sergeant Wilfred Gosselin perhaps best summed it up when he stated: "I'm not saying this is a monster or anything else, but there is something out there, and it's no animal that belongs in the northern part of this state." At the time of the sightings, witnesses were quickly brought to the public's attention through the news media.

The following article appeared on the front page of the Glens Falls *Post-Star*, August 30, 1976:

OFFICERS TRACK CREATURE

Whitehall — Police are investigating reports of a large, unidentified creature seen last week in the town of Whitehall. The first sighting of the creature, which some have referred to as the notorious "Bigfoot," was reported last Tuesday by Marty Paddock of Whitehall and Paul Gosselin of Low Hampton.

They were starting out on a camping trip in the Abair Road vicinity when Paddock spotted a huge shape on the side of the road.

They returned to the area twice, reportedly seeing the creature on the third visit as it moved through a field toward Paddock's truck. Paddock said they left and returned later with a friend and that all three men saw it on that trip, after which they reported the incident to the Whitehall Police.

Whitehall Police, New York State Police and a Washington County Deputy Sheriff all responded to the scene and searched the area, but were only able to spot the creature from a distance.

Although descriptions vary somewhat, the creature has been widely described by both police officials and civilians as between seven and eight feet tall, very hairy, having pink or red eyes, being afraid of light and as weighing between 300 and 400 pounds.

It reportedly makes a sound that has been described as a loud pig squeal or a woman's scream, or a combination.

The creature also walks upright, rather than on all fours, which has resulted in the eyewitnesses ruling out the possibility that the mysterious creature was a bear....

. . . [Whitehall Police Sergeant Wilfred Gosselin] reported that the creature has not hurt any humans but said it was possible it had killed a deer found in the meadow there.

Brian Gosselin, the sergeant's son and Paul's older brother, a patrolman on the Whitehall force, said he saw the creature on Wednesday.

He said the creature came within twenty-five feet of his squad car before a state trooper flashed a light in the creature's eyes. Gosselin said the light caused the creature to cover its eyes and run away screaming.

A newspaper article describing what transpired on August 24, 1976, was sent to Russ Kinne, an internationally known nature photographer and author. He wrote an article for the *Smithsonian Magazine* in 1974, entitled, "The Search Goes On," pertaining to Bigfoot in the Pacific Northwest. Kinne was following up on a story in Watertown, New York, where footprints were found two months earlier. Fifteen-inch tracks were found. Two boys saw an eight-foot, black, hair-covered creature at sunrise. Minutes later they saw it again, walking through a field.

Russ and Jane Kinne, after investigating the Watertown incident, decided to fly in and talk with Paul Gosselin. They phoned him on October 2, and asked if he would meet with them on October 3 at the nearby Fair Haven, Vermont airstrip. I drove Paul to that meeting. It was a warm, clear October day. We were standing there not knowing what Russ Kinne would look like, when we heard a voice say, "You look like you're waiting for someone . . . are you Paul Gosselin?" After the introductions, he invited us to fly in his private plane, the "Tail Dragger." The man was certainly flamboyant.

Sitting in the cockpit waiting for take-off, he pulled out a little booklet and held it up in such a manner that we were able to read the cover, entitled "How to Fly"! Jane remarked, "He likes pulling that on people who've never flown before." Once aloft, Paul served as a guide, instructing Kinne to fly along the Poultney River. The foliage was at its peak, displaying a panorama of color and beauty. Below, the shadow of the "Tail Dragger" merged with the colorful landscape. Then, Paul pointed out Carver's Falls as a reference to a footprint found nearby.

Our pilot banked his plane to the right on a 45 degree angle, opened the window and took a series of pictures. We were planning to visit the cave beneath the falls later. Small talk continued between us, and Russ told us that while flying down through the river valley of Northern California, the thought crossed his mind that you could hide a herd of elephants in any square mile of that country with no trouble. By now, we were returning to the airstrip and I'd been getting a little green around the gills, not accustomed to flying in a small aircraft and trying to keep my stomach from doing anything crazy.

Russ asked what we planned on using to make a cast? "Plaster is too heavy to backpack," he continued. "What I've found better is 'Pour and Place' foam that works pretty good. It's terribly fragile. I have a footprint that I cast three years ago from Washington State and it's in pretty good shape yet. Unfortunately, there's no money appropriated to do a thorough scientific search for Bigfoot." Then, jokingly, he remarked that there's always money available for such things like a study of the calluses on a banjo picker's hand down in the Appalachians. One of these days, someone will get a really good picture and it will be a whole new ballgame.

Once we had landed, we promptly began storing our gear for the hike to Carver's Falls. Russ called out, "Hold on while I grab a couple of cameras and then we're on our way." Paul selected a nature trail that was used by deer and other wildlife. Then he pointed out where the footprint was near the creek bed.

Jane Kinne questioned Paul: "If someone was trying to fake something, would this be a likely spot for someone to find it?" It's not an area normally used by most people, although [there are] some that go Walleye fishing in the Spring, while others hunt here in the Fall. The field that the creature was seen in is not more than a mile and a half from where the footprint was found. It was two sizes larger than a man's and you could make out two toe impressions, but that's all.

We entered the limestone cave that was formed from water belching from the interior. The entrance was rather large, but quickly funnelled inward, where a second, smaller opening dropped off to the left. There was no need to go any further. Russ quickly pointed out that the cave from here on in was too small to house what we were looking for.

Kinne has engaged in extensive work photographing the caves of Trinidad, and the insect and animal life that occupy them. Both he and his long-time friend, Peter Byrne, were honored in 1974 by The Explorer's Club of New York. Byrne is best known for many years as being a Bigfoot Investigator within the Pacific Northwest.

Kinne is a master photographer who specializes in camera traps. In other words, animals manipulated into taking their own pictures. He had planned on using this technique in Oregon on a frozen lake, and using his plane to fly over. If footprints were spotted he would land and check the camera. "That's something I would like to try here," he continued. "If you could spot tracks from the air and they look hot, we could return on skis." Unfortunately, over the years, Russ Kinne has not been able to return to the Adirondacks, but still stays informed of the current sightings.

References:

1. According to Bill Brann, most sightings, including the Abair reports, reveal *no* signs of a hoax. For this to be so, given all of the witnesses, it would have to be a deception of monumental proportions. Of course, there are a few documented cases in New York State of Bigfoot-related hoaxes. Probably the best-known case of fraudulent deception occurred on the Fourth of July morning, 1879, along the west shore of Cayuga Lake in the Finger Lakes Region. Word of a fantastic find had swept through the countryside. Word quickly spread that a petrified man, giant-sized, had been unearthed by a

gang of workmen while widening a roadway leading to the Taughannock House. Reports were impressive! The stone giant weighed an estimated 800 pounds, was nearly seven feet tall, and had an enormous shoulder-span.

The discovery was described as "a human figure lying on its back, arms nearly straight and the legs crossed at the ankle . . . well proportioned with the exception of the feet, which appear more like those of an ape." One newspaper correspondent wrote: "About 40 physicians have examined it, some very carefully, and more than 30 of them believe it the remains of a human being. Yet there are those who believe it a fraud."

The hoax was dreamed up by Ira Dean who made the giant in the cellar of his Trumansburg home. It took him the better part of the winter. He spent hours reading chemistry, for he was determined to combine in the stone man, elements found in the human body. After sculpting the giant, he placed a rock typical of the area, in the crotch of the giant's crossed legs. The rock played a major role in misguiding the scientists, for they exclaimed over the fact that there, encrusted to the figure was a rock uniquely local. After the stone giant was proved a fake, Ira Dean once told a friend, "I always wanted to fool somebody good." This story gives us a good idea to what extremes that some people are willing to go to deceive. The story was drawn from an article by Lois O'Conner, "A Giant Discovery," appearing in the *Ithaca Grapevine*. July 3, 1979, to mark the 100th anniversary of the Taughannock giant's discovery.

Chapter 4

BEYOND ABAIR

The 1976 Abair Road incident in Whitehall was a landmark case for Bigfoot activity in New York. Yet, it was only the tip of an iceberg in a chain of events occurring years before and persisting to this day.

John Green's outstanding book, *Sasquatch: The Apes Among Us*, mentions three New York encounters between December 1974 and January 1975.[1]

In Richmondtown, two boys, aged eleven and twelve, reported a "big (black) furry thing" which made a "loud roar" at about 4:15 p.m. on December 7, 1974 as they were ascending a wooded knoll in back of St. Andrews Episcopal Church parking lot. After hearing the roar, they turned to see a six-foot-tall creature with raised arms. Interpreting the gesture as threatening, they ran off. A subsequent police investigation found nothing.[2]

In January 1975, a five-foot creature "just walking and swinging its arms" was reported by Steven Rich, Jerry Emerson and a Massachusetts boy, along State Street Hill in Watertown.[3]

And a nurse driving on Richmond Road in Richmondtown, braked to avoid hitting a large black hairy creature not far from St. Andrews Episcopal Church. The incident occurred on January 21, 1975 and was reported about 10:45 p.m. The car stopped within six feet of it, as the creature seemed oblivious to the vehicle and walked out of the church parking lot to the churchyard entrance. It had long hair, was about five feet nine inches tall and its arms hung slightly ahead of its body. A pair of four-toed tracks, ten inches long were located nearby.[4]

Just after midnight the next day a couple reportedly saw a bear-like entity in the parking lot, but the witnesses could not be found.[5] The area behind the church is composed of a large swamp and a garbage dump.[6]

Some time in the 1970s, before the State had banned planes landing on its lakes and ponds, outdoorsman Jim Caruso used to hire an Adirondack bush pilot to fly him back into the interior on fishing trips. The pilot told Caruso of an incident while flying over a mountain range that had been lumbered off. He saw "this thing" in the clearing. Thinking it was a bear, he circled back for a closer look just in time to see the creature run off on two legs disappearing into the tall timber.[7]

Long after the excitement over the Abair Road incident had subsided, another encounter was brought to light in Whitehall by Skene Valley Country Club owner Clifford Sparks. The former dairy farmer who later turned his spread into a popular golf course, came public with an incident which happened to him in May 1975.

Sparks described seeing a seven to eight-foot-tall "sloth-like thing." He was working on the greens about 11:30 at night in his electric golf cart by the first green adjacent to a wooded area. Suddenly "this great big hairy thing was silhouetted against the moonlit skyline." It had a very big girth and was very tall. When it caught a glimpse of Sparks, he said: "I think it was a lot more startled than I was," although he noted, "The hair on the back of my neck stood right up, because these carts don't go very fast."

He described its head as "egg" or "cone-shaped." He continued: "It lumbered and walked with a very clumsy gait. . . . The creature had a different knee and leg action than a man . . . I don't know how, just different."[8] Its shoulders were not very wide and "it didn't seem to have much of a neck." The creature (about 35 feet away) reportedly ran from the green and "crashed" through the woods in an awkward manner, making much noise.[9]

A couple of years after the incident, Sparks said he was standing outside the country club at 4 a.m. with friend Rolly Neddo, also of Whitehall, when they heard "one hell of a blood-curdling squeal." It was very "high-pitched" and lasted several seconds. Needless to say, the pair didn't investigate further.[10]

Despite his frightening experience, Sparks is sentimental: "I don't think they should shoot it . . . because as far as I know, it hasn't ever hurt anyone."

One night in June 1975, near Saranac Lake, two Watertown residents said they were driving on Route 3 and saw a "Bigfoot" squatting beside the road as they rounded a turn. One of the witnesses told investigator Milton LaSalle that the creature then stood and walked off into the nearby brush.[11] In the 1920's, an elderly couple by the name of Wright would not allow their grandchildren to play in back of their home or barns. A relative told investigator Bill Brann that there was what they described as a strange bear that walked upright and roamed freely on their property.

During the fall of that year, Whitehall Police Sgt. Wilfred Gosselin said he was hunting one night with his brother Russell at the junction of Rt. 22A and Abair Road when he heard an "eerie, high-pitched yell" that lasted for about a minute. Wilfred said that some nearby cows ran frantically from the field and "my brother Russell came out of there as white as a sheet."[12]

On September 1, 1976, a Granville man rushed into the Whitehall police station proclaiming, "I shot Bigfoot." The dispatcher on duty that evening was Robert Martell. "He was scared," said Martell, who quickly became convinced of his sincerity. Sgt. Wilfred Gosselin officially logged the incident as follows: "Frank McFarren of Granville came and reported that at 11:10 PM he shot four .12 gau[ge] rifle slugs and six to eight .22 rifle bullets at a huge creature that came at him at C[arvers] Falls Road. Notified N[ew York] S[tate] police."

The man was accompanied by others when they engaged the creature. New York State Troopers and off-duty Whitehall Police responded to the scene, but no further sightings were made that evening. Officials did find a used shotgun shell at the site, but nothing more. Unable to do much more than search the area, authorities simply noted the incident and left.[13]

While many locals remain skeptical of this incident, other

New York reports were coming in. Ten days later a pair of teenage boys said they heard strange screams, then saw a hulking figure twice during the twilight hours in a wooded area a few miles from Watertown, several hundred miles west of Whitehall. It was August 11, when according to an interview with investigator Milton LaSalle, the pair claimed to have had encounters with a large black, hair-covered creature several miles east of Watertown. While walking on Overlook Drive around five a.m., thumping noises and screams were heard for some fifteen minutes in a brush-filled area. At about 5:45 a.m. a large, black, hairy figure was seen in the road. After yelling at it, the creature ran away in an erect position. Later that morning they saw it again from a friend's house. It was described as eight feet tall, with broad shoulders and a big build.[14]

Later that year, in the fall, a coon hunter from Oxbow was reportedly startled by a heavy-set hairy creature that ran upright across an open area in the full monnlight.[15]

Sixty-five-year-old Royal Bennett and his granddaughter Shannon, in March 1977, had a sighting in a clearing near Fish Hill Road in a meadow on the west side of South Bay, near Whitehall. According to Mr. Bennett, "My fourteen-year-old granddaughter and I like to step out on the back porch and focus our binoculars on the clearing and watch for deer. At this time of the year, they would come to get the apples in a few old apple trees that remained there."

"I was focusing on what I thought to be a stump . . . suddenly it stood up and with a few quick strides, it had crossed the clearing out of sight. At first, I thought it was a snake hunter [rattlesnake], but quickly realized it couldn't be at this time of the year. If it was a man, it was an awfully big man . . . it looked honey-colored. I love the woods. I've never been afraid to go in them. I have never seen anything in there that would bother me. I would have to believe that thing wouldn't bother you."

"Even from this distance with the aid of binoculars, I could tell it would weigh close to 500 pounds and it was tall. . . . It's close to 100 feet across that clearing. No bear can walk that far on its hind legs, and . . . it was the wrong color for a bear."

Shannon described the sighting: "It didn't move terribly fast. It looked like it was a little hunched over when it moved and light tan in color on the main part of the body. It was about one in the afternoon when we saw it. We couldn't see the face clearly, it was just too far away. I would estimate the height between seven and eight feet tall and it had long arms that swung as it walked. Then it entered the trees near the clearing. At first I thought it was a person, but as I watched it, I could tell it wasn't. Last winter, when my grandfather and I were out snowmobiling off in the [nearby] Diameter, we saw [ten] large tracks in the snow. The stride was farther apart than what a man could do. My sixteen-year-old brother, a year and a half before, was walking his girlfriend home when they heard a loud, weird scream. . . . He never saw it, but he heard it running off. It sounded like it was running off on two legs within a heavily wooded, rocky area."[16]

The family had no way of knowing that a small team of investigators was formed and had located a large track about five miles from where their sighting occurred. On March 3, 1977, at Pine Lake, northwest of Whitehall, Bill Brann, Dick Newman, Clifford South and John King discovered a 13¼-inch impression embedded in a swampy area known as The Diameter. Brann was able to make a plaster casting of the print, which displayed an unusual curvature. A three-week search by the group yielded no further evidence.[17]

A large hairy creature was reported on two occasions by two separate pairs of railway employees near Theresa, New York on June 27 and 28. In each instance, the sighting ended with the figure diappearing into the bushes. Large human-shaped prints with five toes were also reported at both locations.[18]

In July 1977, a couple (who like most Bigfoot witnesses, wish to remain anonymous) and their three children were camping in a remote section of northern Saratoga County called Big Eddy, along the west branch of the Sacandaga River. The family dog had acted up during the night, whimpering uncharacteristically. The man stated:

"The next morning I left the campsite to go off fishing. I entered this ravine. It was very eerie. There were no signs of birds or other wildlife; unusually still. . . . I felt like I was being watched. I noticed in the mud a large footprint about fourteen inches long to six inches wide. The toes were big on the end and narrow in the middle. Otherwise, it looked like a human footprint. I wondered who the hell would be running around way out here barefoot. There [are] no good swimming holes along the stream. Then I noticed more tracks in the mud and they didn't resemble bear tracks."

"I know how my wife and kids would have reacted if I told them about the tracks I'd seen along the trail. I waited until after we hiked back to the car, two miles from where we were camped. When I told my wife about the tracks I'd seen, that's when she informed me she'd seen large tracks around the camp also."[19]

Two deputy sheriffs from Saratoga County, one an investigating officer and the other his back-up, recorded an unusual incident one summer in the late 1970s. The officer, on arriving, saw a number of people milling about the dwelling. He asked what was the problem and was told something was screaming at the rear of the trailer and had pulled a tree ten inches in diameter from the ground and hurled it against the mobile home. The officer went around back. Indeed there was a tree leaning up against the trailer. There was thick brush nearby with indications that something quite large and powerful had walked through it. The investigating officer followed the trail for a distance and saw nothing. Returning, he advised residents to lock their doors and windows. He then called the dispatcher, advising him of the conditions that he found.

Dispatcher: "Bob, have you been drinking?"

The investigating officer requested a wildlife biologist be sent to the area in the morning. Jim, the back-up deputy remarked: "I know what happened. I listened to the entire conversation."[20]

The corner of Abair Road and Rt. 22A in Whitehall (the scene of two previous encounters), was also the site of an eerie encounter with something in early August 1978. A man living in the area at the time says that he was awakened by whining yelps from his Doberman pinscher at about 1 a.m. To his amazement, the dog was hiding under the bed. The man, who wishes anonimity, said: "I mean, he was really terrified. He was a very ferocious and fearless dog. He would attack a bull and not back off." But on this night the normally fearless dog was "terrified, trying to crawl under the bed and get away." The man sat on his bed, peering out the window, his .22 caliber rifle cocked with his finger on the trigger.

Then came the most frightening part, he recalls. A loud piercing scream shattered the calm of that hot, humid night, sending involuntary shivers up and down his spine. He said it sounded like "an anguished cry, like somebody going through ultimate pain. This was a very lonely, painful shrieking and it echoed terrible." Very familiar with animals in the area, he said emphatically that no animal ever sounded like that. The witness also reported that an elderly woman living within a half-mile of the sighting claimed to have heard shrieking cries on many occasions.[21]. When Bob Bartholomew contacted the woman, she denied ever having made the statement.[22]

The 1980s greeted Bigfoot researchers with a healthy dose of new encounters. On June 4, 1980, thirty-four-year-old Red Ranaudo of Connecticut was camping in the rugged woods of Lawrenceburg, New York. "I lit a fire, my truck was parked beside me and I was sort of laying there in my sleeping bag. I was on some sort of a knob, a high part of the terrain. Down below me toward the road was a creek and a beaver pond. I let the fire go out and I went to sleep." The peaceful tranquility of the night woods was casually interrupted by what Ranaudo took to be the cries of a wolf or coy dog. "I sat upright and was looking around. There was no moon, but all the stars were out. I didn't have my glasses on but I could see pretty well. I'd been awake for a while and my eyes were adjusted to the night. Loud crashing sounds came from nearby brush."

"I was sitting up and I turned around to look in the field and I heard this thing coming through the underbursh. It was making loud thuds. I could hear it coming for quite a distance before I saw it, but finally I saw this white shape coming out of the darkness. It was walking at a pretty good pace, but the thing was that it was breathing real hard, like it had asthma, or it had been running real hard. There were big heavy noises . . . very loud . . . fifty to seventy-five yards away."

Ranaudo managed to get a good look. " . . . this thing was

big. It was large and white . . . and furry. I was looking at it pretty closely and even though I couldn't see it that clearly, I definitely had a feeling about what it was. Anyway, I got into the truck. I rolled the window down and stuck my head out and I could see it fading back into the darkness. And then it disappeared and I didn't hear it anymore."

Ranuado and the owner of the site returned to the spot days later. Footprints were found and casts measuring fifteen inches in length were made. He later told a reporter: "I'd just assume they leave him alone. I know I believe it. I don't really care if anyone else believes it."[23]

A young man cross country skiing within the Adirondack Park in winter 1981, found a trail of oversized footprints as far as the eye could see, apparently left by something that walked upright. Using a ski pole as a reference, he placed it between the tracks. The distance between the prints was greater than the length of the pole. The man took photos, but they have not been made available.[24] Also in 1982, northwest of Indian Lake, on Bullhead Mountain, Hamilton County, a hunter was told of another set of large tracks he had seen. He didn't believe they were bear tracks. The next day the hunter decided to look for himself. Having tracked bear in Canada, he was capable of differentiating between bear tracks and something else.

Climbing to the summit of Bullhead, elevation 3,553 feet, he found a hut ten feet in diameter, about four feet high, dome-shaped with a large opening. It was constructed of hand-broken branches and trees as big around as broom handles. "It would take quite a man to accomplish that," he remarked. From the hut's opening he followed tracks eighteen inches long and approximately eight inches wide at the toes for over a mile that seemed to just shuffle along with an increasing stride. The prints were clearly clawless; this was no bear. The tracks led to a narrow ridge on the side of a cliff then dropped off about one hundred feet.

"I decided not to pursue it in case it decided to turn around and come back and I'd find myself with no place to go." A few days later flying over the area viewing the prints along the ridge, he saw they did not double back. At the advice of the pilot, they didn't fly any closer, afraid of a possible down draft. With the aid of binoculars, he stated, "I don't see how anything could have climbed its way out of there."[25]

The next major incident was reported back in Whitehall, when two law enforcement officials wishing to keep their identities secret, told Paul Bartholomew they were driving north at about 4:30 a.m. in early February 1982, when a large hairy creature made a "dash" across Rt. 22, a few hundred feet in front of the Washington County Highway Department garage. The creature reportedly made its way up a steep embankment and disappeared into a heavily wooded area.

They described the ape-like creature as being 7½ to 8 feet tall, all covered with a very dark brown fur that appeared dirty and mangy. "There's no way in hell that I could believe this was a man in a fur suit," the first officer exclaimed. He described it as having long arms that swung from side to side with movements similar to that of a person, as it took "big, lengthy strides." It moved "like a scared rabbit" at a pace "a relay runner would have trouble keeping up with." Its shoulders were apparently not very broad. The creature was tall and lanky, its eyes highly reflective. The first officer said that he stopped the car, got out and followed after it as it headed up into the mountainous woods. He said the creature "slouched" and had "poor posture for a human."

When the first officer was tracking after the mysterious creature, the second said that he was perfectly content to stay in the car and watch from a distance.

Both officers say they are fearful of ridicule and of damaging their reputations and credibility if they come forward publicly, but both offered to take polygraph tests to indicate their sincerity.[26]

The second officer also says that four years earlier he encountered a similar creature between May 15 and 20 at 7:30 p.m. in a field in the Town of Whitehall. When the creature spotted him "it turned right around and got the hell out of there," he said.[25]

The following year, an Associated Press report told of a Bigfoot-like creature in Jefferson County.

> Dexter, NY (AP) — It's summer and Bigfoot is back in the North Country. Jefferson County officials say a Dexter resident reported spotting a hairy, 7-foot creature earlier this week near a hardware store in Dexter.[28]

A reporter with a sense of humor at WGY radio in Schenectady footnoted the Dexter sighting by speculating that because it was seen near a hardware store, perhaps it was looking for "a monkey wrench."[29]

Lake George in Warren County is known for being one of the most popular lakes within the Adirondacks. What is not known is that on October 7, 1983, between 7:30 and 8 p.m., three young men (from ages fifteen to twenty-seven), reported a brief encounter with a possible Bigfoot creature near French Mountain. They were four miles south of Lake George Village on a popular bike trail when they heard something screaming at the top of the hill. When the older of the three flashed a light in the direction of the vocalizations, he saw large red eyes reflecting in the light, seven feet off the ground.

"It didn't take us long to get back to the [nearby] city of Glens Falls," said one witness. "It really scared us. The following day we returned to the spot where we'd seen it and there was a strong stench still in the air, and the smell did not resemble that of a skunk." The mother of the fifteen-year-old confirmed that the trio was genuinely frightened.[30]

Also in October, Richard Newman and his fifteen-year-old son, Eric, were fishing at Moose Mountain Pond in Essex County near North Hudson. At dusk they heard loud crunching sounds from the woods directly behind their tent. "We went to investigate," said Newman. "My son spotted two large hairy legs running off to the left of us. The next day we were hiking out and we met two men working an old log road. I told them what my son saw; two large black hairy legs about three feet long. By the looks on their faces, they accepted the fact that it had only two legs. I believe the two men were trying to bring out the point. At three feet, Eric would have seen some of the lower body if it had been a bear."[31]

The year 1984 saw a resurgence of Bigfoot activity in the Whitehall area. On Thursday evening, May 10, the tranquil atmosphere at Spark's Skene Valley Country Club was suddenly interrupted by a series of bizarre "laughing sounds" which remain unexplained. Owner Clifford Sparks, wife Pat and three regulars were chatting when at about 10:30 p.m. a very loud and distant laughing sound sliced through the walls of the club.

"Everyone just stopped talking and listened," said Pat.

The strange vocalization lasted but a few seconds, but memories of the eerie sound will likely stay imprinted in the minds of those present forever. "I'm going to call this place Spooksville instead of Sparks," joked a genuinely frightened customer. Sparks, familiar with electrical equipment used by bands which sometimes play at the club, was particularly impressed by the decibel level. He believes the volume and pitch of the sound could not be duplicated by equipment. [32]

The mystery deepened the next evening when shortly after 11 p.m. at least four workers for the Whitehall Junior and Senior High School, only a few hundred yards from the golf course, heard a similar type of vocalization. "It was such a severe laughing sound . . . it scared the living heck out of me . . . my hair just stood right up on end, that's all I can say. I have never heard another sound like that . . . I just don't know what it is," said Connie Prefountaine. She was working with another woman at the Elementary School when they heard the bizarre vocal display. "It was such a severe laughing, horrible sound . . . stupid . . . childish . . . I'm scared to be up here alone." [33]

The next reported vocalization was heard by a young woman living at the base of Black Mountain. She says that on the evening of June 20, a "horrendous shriek" echoed across the Black Mountain Base Trail and lasted but a few seconds. [34]

Another eerie sound was heard in the same vicinity by William "Bud" Manell one afternoon in early August. Manell was operating the Whitehall dump (surrounded by a large marsh) at East Bay when he was chilled by a "scream going into a raging screech," lasting only seconds. [35]

A few days later about twenty miles away, a strange sound was heard in Hartford, by a man and several neighbors. It was described as like a "woman in labor." It was "high-pitched" and "real eerie." The sounds seemed to cross the man's lawn before heading into the nearby woods.

The man said the sounds came in "long stretches," driving area dogs crazy with excitement. He added that practically "the whole town heard it." The man has lived in Hartford for fifteen years, hunting and fishing extensively yet said he has never heard anything like it before.[36]

During a three-day period from August 15 to 17, 1984, unusual vocalizations were heard by a Whitehall family generally between 10:30 p.m and 12:30 a.m. One described them as like an animal caught in a trap undergoing agonizing pain. Another described the sounds as starting out like a dog, then developing into a long "siren" type noise stretching out for as long as a minute.

It wasn't until August 20 that one man found the possible source of the vocalizations. At about 10:45 p.m., a seven to eight-foot-tall upright figure was seen at a distance of some twenty yards. After viewing the creature, he quickly turned to get a friend's attention, but it was too late. Upon turning back, it was gone.

A second sighting was made by the same man eight days later not far from the original spot. At about 8:30 p.m., a 7½ to 8-foot-tall creature was seen walking near a house. An outside light emitted enough light to enable the frightened man to see a huge creature "at least 400 pounds." The sighting lasted ten seconds before the creature was seen running off.[37]

Reports of eerie nocturnal vocalizations have been continuously reported to this day. They are too numerous to cover case by case. But the next major sightings were to take place in August 1989. Paul Bartholomew detailed one of these incidents in a front-page story for the *Whitehall Times* of September 7:

> A startled teenager may have recently glimpsed a creature resembling the legendary "Bigfoot" or "Sasquatch" in Hampton, New York.
>
> The 16-year-old, wishing to remain anonymous, claims he was walking along 22A South when he spotted a dark figure lurking along the roadside. The sighting reportedly took place around 3 PM on August 18.
>
> The youth reportedly observed the creature for approximately three full seconds before both took off in opposite directions.
>
> "I could see the back, a big back, and it was dark, it

was awful matted and scruffy-like," said the witness.

The youth was accompanied by a dog which apparently reacted to the presence of something.

"The dog . . . came across the road near where the thing was standing and it started whining and took off," said the teen.

On August 24, the mystery deepened as the young man and a friend camped out near where the sighting took place. At 2 AM it seemed that something was watching them.

"I stared at it and it stared back and it kind of went away," the youth said.

The witness said he observed two "glowing red eyes" approximately six feet off the ground. The eyes appeared to be circling the camp.

"They just weren't round like, they were oblong, longer than they were round," added the observer.

The youth contacted Dr. Warren Cook, Professor of History and Anthropology at Castelton State College (Vermont) and noted authority on Bigfoot. Dr. Cook contacted fortean researcher, Paul B. Bartholomew, who investigated the sightings.

Two possible footprints were found at the campsite in direct relation to where the "glowing red eyes" were observed. The clearer of the two impressions measured 10½ inches long by 4½ inches wide, with a stride of 56 inches between them.

It is interesting to note that the date of this sighting falls on the thirteenth anniversary of the Abair Road, Whitehall, New York sightings of 1976. In that instance as many as nine witnesses, many of them law enforcement officials, reported seeing a large, hairy, red-eyed creature walking on two legs and disappearing into the dense rural woodlands.

Dr. Cook feels the timing of the sightings are probably not coincidental.

"If these creatures do migrate and feel comfortable and safe traveling a particular route, then it makes sense that they would stay along the same routes," said Cook.

On August 28, high-pitched screams were heard coming from the woods at about 1 a.m. Lasting 30 seconds, with four seconds separating each scream, the mystery vocalizations echoed through Hampton for at least three minutes.[38]

That same month, an Averill Park couple were driving along a rural road just outside of Postenkill when they spotted a large, running creature. They related their experience in a letter to Paul Bartholomew:

> Upon rounding a bend in the road we both observed a large upright figure vault a pasture fence approximately 100 feet ahead of our vehicle. This figure was tall and reddish blonde in color and running very quickly. It was in the path of my headlights only for a moment. I was traveling approximately 35 mph., and by the time we proceeded to the area where we first saw this thing . . . we could still make out a figure running upright downhill across a pasture. I did slow down but not stop. I had no immediate logical explanation for what we had just witnessed, and experienced a feeling of absolute fear and dumbfoundedness difficult to describe.

Ghent, New York was the location where large tracks were found in January 1990. The incident was described to Bruce Hallenbeck by a highly credible witness preferring anonymity, who found the trail stretching across a snow-covered field. The prints measured over twenty inches in length. Days later, in the same area, the man's son found similar tracks, which disappeared into a thicket.[40]

In July, three anonymous witnesses reported seeing a "tall, big, dark" figure as it crossed a field off County Route 21 in Whitehall, New York.[41] In fact, sightings have continued into 1991. In March, Herbert Francisco of Greece, New York found several oversized human-like tracks in the vicinity of Loon Lake Mountain in the Adirondacks while visiting his former brother-in-law and wife. The prints measured eighteen to twenty-two inches long, with a ten-foot stride. He believes the creature was running since the heel was deeper than the ball of the foot. Francisco adds that his hosts have been hearing powerful screams and high-pitched yelps in the same area.[42]

During early April, Katherine Kaifer reported a Bigfoot sighting in the vicinity of Long Lake, about forty miles south of Loon Lake Mountain.

It is interesting to note that certain areas have higher concentrations of sightings. One such locale is the Kinderhook, New York region, about fifteen miles south of Albany. Some residents have seen what has been dubbed "The Kinderhook Creature," which is the focus of Chapter 5.

References:

1. Green, John, *Sasquatch: The Apes Among Us*. Seattle, WA: Hancock House, 1978, pp. 233-234.
2. Ibid., p. 233.
3. Ibid., p. 233-234, citing the *Watertown Daily Times*, August 2, 1977. An interview with the witnesses was conducted by Milton LaSalle of Watertown.
4. Ibid., p. 233.
5. Ibid., p. 233.
6. Ibid., p. 233.
7. Based on a 1983 personal interview by Jim Caruso, supplied to Bill Brann.
8. Bill Brann notes that: Clifford Sparks' description of what he saw that night was pear-shaped, narrow through the shoulders, with the bulk of the animal being along its hips. Archie Buckley, a California Bigfoot investigator points out in a paper that was published in *The Sasquatch and Other Unknown Homonids*, that "body hair, and their tremendous gluteal muscles (buttocks), give an underslung appearance, particularly, when viewed from an uphill or downhill position." According to Buckley, "Mr. Sparks may have given us another piece of evidence when he stated, 'the creature had a different knee and leg action than a man.' Sparks using his body to characterize movement, stated, 'the knee action was different, I don't know how, just different.' That impressed me."

In a letter to me (Bill Brann) dated March 6, 1987, Buckley assured me that his findings are based on years of field research on the flex-knee gait. Could this be what Mr. Sparks noted when he encountered the creature? Buckley states in his paper, 'Report on Sasquatch Field Findings,' Sasquatch's lower extremities, including ankles and feet, are big because of the heavy weight that must be supported as a bipedal over a mountainous terrain. Couple this with hair and a flex-knee gait and one can easily misinterpret when viewing Patterson's film that weight bearing is more toward the center of the foot than in man's. The primary reason for this misleading conclusion is their flex-knee gait. . . .

As I indicated initially, this gait is the smoothest and most efficient that we humans can use in the mountains. It is, and I repeat, biomechanically sound. In such a gait, both the arm swing and stride are naturally increased for better balance on horizontal and incline planes. This brings into play an increased range of all the powerful extensors of these joints. It thus allows for greater muscular movement, strength, control and balance than the normal so-called human gait, where in each step we roll over the hip and momentarily decrease control and balance until the opposite foot makes contact. In fact, we are in a sense, falling forward until contact is made. In a flex-knee gait not only is the stride length increased, but both feet are generally in contact with the soil; as one foot pushes off, the heel of the opposite is already in contact. It results in a smooth fluid method of walking that the ambulator is in control of at all times. The increased arm swing is fundamental to balance because of the longer stride. In no way is it over-exaggerated and self-conscious movement, as referred to by Napier.

Mr. Buckley is co-founder of the California Bay Area Group made up of dedicated Sasquatch researchers.

9. Interview between Cliff Sparks and Bob Bartholomew, Fall 1984, and subsequent interviews by Paul Bartholomew and Bill Brann.

10. Based on a series of interviews with Clifford Sparks by Paul Bartholomew.

11. Green, John, *Sasquatch: The Apes Among Us*. Seattle, WA: Hancock House, 1978, p. 234. Based on an interview between Milton LaSalle and one of the witnesses, a man.

12. Based on a series of interviews between Wilfred Gosselin and Paul and Bob Bartholomew and Bill Brann.

13. Interview between Paul Bartholomew and Whitehall Police Dispatcher Robert Martell. Also, interview between Bob Bartholomew and Whitehall Police Dispatcher, Fred Palmer.

14. Green, John, *Sasquatch; The Apes Among Us*. Seattle, WA: Hancock House, 1978, p. 234. Based on an interview between Milton LaSalle and the witnesses.

15. Ibid., p. 235, based on a second-hand story told to Milton LaSalle.

16. Based on a series of interviews between the witnesses and Bill Brann.

17. Data supplied by Bill Brann.

18. Ibid., p. 235, citing the *Watertown Daily Times*, August 2, 1977. Milton LaSalle investigated the case.

19. Based on a series of interviews between the man and Bill Brann.

20. Based on a series of interviews conducted by Bill Brann with officers involved. They feared ridicule if their full names were released.

21. Interviews by Paul and Bob Bartholomew with the man, whom the witnesses have known for several years.

22. Brief telephone conversation between the elderly woman and Bob Bartholomew, Fall 1984.

23. "Local Man Spots Bigfoot in NY State—An Encounter With a Yeti," *Newton Bee*, CT, June 22, 1984, by Curtiss Clark, pp. 19-20.

24. Based on an interview between Bill Brann and the boy's father.

25. Based on information and interviews conducted by Bill Brann.

26. Based on a series of interviews between the officers and Paul Bartholomew. The officers drove Paul to the site on more than one occasion to reconstruct the incident.

27. Interviews by Paul Bartholomew and the anonymous officer.

28. "Big, Hairy Creature Spied," Glens Falls, NY *Post-Star*, August 5, 1983, by the Associated Press.
29. From Bob Bartholomew, who then worked as "North Country Correspondent" for WGY radio, Schenectady, NY.
30. Based on a series of personal interviews by Bill Brann.
31. Personal interviews by Bill Brann.
32. Personal interviews by Paul Bartholomew.
33. Personal interviews by Paul Bartholomew with the witness.
34. Based on a report given to the late editor/publisher of *The Independent* newspaper, Whitehall, NY, Rev. George Greenough.
35. Personal interviews with the man by Paul Bartholomew and Bill Brann.
36. Based on interviews by Paul Bartholomew with the witnesses.
37. Paul Bartholomew interview with the family.
38. The article was based on a series of interviews by Paul Bartholomew and Dr. Warren Cook.
39. Based on a letter to Paul Bartholomew from the couple.
40. From interviews conducted by Bruce Hallenbeck.
41. Based on a report supplied to Paul Bartholomew.
42. Telephone conversation between Bill Brann and Herbert Francisco.
43. Bill Brann learned of this encounter from the witness who called the "800" *Fate* Magazine hotline.

Chapter 5

THE KINDERHOOK CREATURE

One of the most haunted places in New York State's Hudson Valley is the tiny town of Kinderhook, located in northern Columbia County. The name means "Children's Corner" in Dutch, and, appropriately enough, it was in Kinderhook that Washington Irving gathered material for his classic tale, *The Legend of Sleepy Hollow*.

Kinderhook is steeped in history and folklore of this sort, and often the two intermingle to the point where they become virtually indistinguishable from one another—headless horsemen, ghostly schoolmasters and wandering presidents (Martin Van Buren, eighth president of the United States was born and buried here, and his ghost reputedly haunts the vicinity), omens of doom and relics of death. Kinderhook and its environs abound in such mysteries. In fact, new strange and mysterious stories are being added all the time.

Kinderhook seems to be the home (or at least gathering place) for a group of Bigfoot-type creatures which are often sighted, heard and tracked. I have made plaster casts of both three and five-toed prints.

Several members of my family have encountered these creatures on occasion. Encounters range from finding footprints and the hearing of strange vocalizations, to actual eyewitness sightings of one or more creatures walking in the woods or along the roadside.

I first heard of "monsters" roaming the Hudson Valley in the mid-70s, and frankly, I was skeptical. It's all very well to have such beasts as the Yeti in Tibet and the Sasquatch romping about in the Pacific Northwest, but such creatures literally in your own backyard? The notion seemed rather silly.

And yet, in 1978, there was an article in the now-defunct *Hudson River Chronicle* concerning sightings of hairy hominids in northern Dutchess County, and also in such Columbia country towns as Canaan, Chatham and Nassau. It was in that same year that strange footprints in the snow were found near my home, and near my parents' home which lies on the edge of a forbidding tract of swampland and forest called Cushing's Hill.

The tracks were three-toed and very large. My cousin, Barry Knights, who was only thirteen at the time, was already an experienced hunter and trapper, and he found a set of three-toed tracks in the snow in December 1978. They were on my own property, crossing a log. I photographed them and sent a copy of the pictures to the *Chronicle*, which promptly lost them—along with the negatives. I was stymied as to what the prints could actually have meant. There were only three, and they seemed to end in the midst of snow. Unless the creature somehow took flight, that seemed physically impossible.

It was in the same month that my grandmother, Martha Hallenbeck, a remarkable, no-nonsense lady, looked out of her kitchen window early one morning and saw what was apparently a large creature curled up and seemingly resting on her lawn. Dawn was just streaking the sky and she couldn't see it clearly, but it looked strange enough to her that she did not immediately come forth with her story for fear of ridicule.

"I didn't tell anyone," she later said, "because I was afraid people would cart me away somewhere. It was only afterward, when other people said they had seen the same things, that I talked about it."

As my grandmother related the story: "There was some big black thing all curled up down at the end of the lawn one morning when I got up really bright and early. And then I saw tracks (in the snow) and I never said a word because I thought they were going to say, 'She's nutty.'"

"I had my garbage in a green bag, the same as I have on the back porch now, only I had it out here by the corner of the house and it used to be (around this time) taken up and set down in the lawn down there, and things were taken out of it."

"The bag wasn't torn. But the food was taken out, and just as though a person took it out or something—nothing like an animal would do, and I kept wondering about that because if the dogs get in it . . . it's all over the place, and this wasn't. It was very neat."

"And my neighbor over here called me after that and she said her garbage that she had in a shed had had the same thing done to it. And she . . . found the empty bag in a tree . . . it was just picked up out of the shed and carried away."

My grandmother, seventy-two at the time of the sighting, described the creature: "I think it had quite long hair. And it was very tall. It was sort of circles, curled up."

That description is often applied to "almas" (the Russian wildman) that have been seen sleeping. American Bigfeet have also been described as sleeping in this almost fetal position.

My grandmother continued: "The one funny thing about that creature, whatever it is, it seems to appear and disappear. One minute it's there and the next minute it's gone. And we have seen tracks leading somewhere and even the tracks seem to stop right there, and you don't see them anymore. That's a mystery. The whole thing is a mystery to me."

There was no particular odor noticed by my grandmother during her 1978 sighting. When she was shown the sketches that Bill Brann and Bob and Paul Bartholomew had shown to Clifford Sparks, she chose sketch number two as being the most like what she had seen. It was the same sketch that Sparks had chosen.

Tracks that my father attributed to a bear were seen all that winter. But my father, who is also a very experienced hunter and woodsman, found something while hunting at the top of Cushing's Hill that winter that was quite unbear-like.

What my father found were three dead rabbits stuffed into the snow at the top of Cushing's Hill, as if they were being stored away for the winter. The curious thing was that there were no tracks nearby at all, and it was in a very remote spot. There was no sign of blood around the rabbits either.

The rest of the winter (and the following spring and summer) were devoid of any "creature" activity in the specific area near Canaan, which borders on Massachusetts. There is an old stretch of road in that area that has seemingly run the gamut of the paranormal: everything has been seen in the nearby woods, from Bigfoot to UFOs to "witch fires" or "fairy lights."

It wasn't until December 5, 1979, that things started happening again in Kinderhook. Once more, the activity seemed to center around Cushing's Hill. This time, the encounter was a visual one by my cousin, Barry.

My grandmother described it best: "My grandson Barry was setting traps one day (in the swampy area near Cushing's Hill, about a mile from my grandparents' house) and he came back and his face was so white—as white as could be—and he said to me, 'Grandma, I saw four great big things crossing the creek and going into the woods down there.' And I'm sure he saw something because I hadn't mentioned anything I'd seen before that. And then I told everyone that I had seen the tracks before."

I was there that afternoon when my cousin came running into the house. He was quite terrified. He had a baseball bat with him and he said that he still hadn't felt safe. He sometimes used the bat to kill an animal (usually muskrat) that he had trapped. But he felt it was no match for whatever it was he had seen. He also remarked that they had made noises, grunting and clacking sounds. As my grandmother so succinctly put it: "So he ran all the way home, and he didn't go trapping there again right away."

What had my cousin seen that scared him so? Although it was daylight, the dense foliage of the swamp partially concealed the creatures, but he described them as light brown, furry things, walking across the creek clacking and grunting as they went. Through the bushes it was difficult to tell, but he was sure that they were big—and at age fourteen, he was a strapping boy of about six feet—and he was equally sure they were walking on two legs.

The day of his sightings, a friend of mine and I decided to investigate the area. We could not get Barry to go into that area again, so my other cousin, Russell, joined us. We didn't find anything on the order of footprints, but we crossed some rough terrain, nearly got stuck in some bogs (there is actually quicksand and a number of dangerous sinkholes in the area) and discovered that a mere mile from home, the area in and around Cushing's Hill seemed to be another world.

April, 1980. One of the best visual sightings we have on record in Columbia County is from a woman whose name is Barbara, but who prefers anonymity to protect herself from the everpresent threat of ridicule. The woman was returning from Albany late one night on Rt. 9. She had just entered Columbia County, and on her right were woods and on her left, an unplanted cornfield.

She saw the thing in the headlights of her car. She described it as being about 7½ feet tall, with reddish brown fur. As she put it: "It looked like a highly evolved ape." The woman slowed her car and watched in disbelief as the creature walked across the road into the cornfield and on out of sight. Unfortunately, she didn't think to look for footprints, and didn't inform anyone about her sighting until nearly a year later. The tracks in the mud must have startled at least one farmer the next morning.

The first time I personally heard what I believe to be the vocalization of the creature was in July of 1980. I was escorting a friend who was visiting from England back to where she was staying. It was about eleven o'clock at night and there was a full moon. Suddenly, from the depths of the forest that encircle our property, we heard the most incredible sound. It was the vocalization of some animal, beginning with a series of grunting noises, turning into a crescendo of shrieking or screaming, and finally dying down in a low moan. It lasted for approximately thrity seconds.

After a moment of shocked silence, my friend turned to me and said, with British understatement: "Is that a typical American sound to hear at night?"

"No!" I assured her. "I never heard that sound before in my life!"

At the time, I was still somewhat skeptical of the possibility of a Bigfoot existing in the area, so I didn't press the issue to investigate the cause of the sound. I knew that my friend wouldn't accompany me anyway, come hell or high water.

It was on the night of September 24, 1980, that I became convinced. It was another full moon night. It was in fact, the biggest and brightest full moon I have ever seen before or since. The moon looked the size of a basketball, almost as though you could reach out and touch it.

My cousin Barry and I had gone for an early evening walk around the golf course nearby as we watched the moon rise. In retrospect, the amazing thing was that we were both making fun of the Bigfoot story as we walked. Even though Barry had seen something really unusual the year before, he was trying to rationalize himself into believing it had been something else—bear, deer, anything he could think of.

But even more strange, looking back at it, was that the whole day had been weird. My entry for September 24 in my diary read: "Incredible day. Walked around the golf course in the afternoon and had the weirdest sensation of being followed by something, but could see nothing unusual. Later, Barry and I walked around the golf course again and heard all the dogs barking their heads off. Went out to Chatham at about 9 p.m., was called by my grandmother who wanted me to come home because there was a "something" outside the house terrifying her. By the time I got home, it was gone."

In fact, by the time I got home, I felt like Richard Dreyfuss in "Close Encounters of the Third Kind." Barry was there with his shotgun, my grandmother was talking excitedly about what had happened, and my aunt Barbara (Barry's mother) was in a state of semi-panic.

What had happened the night of September 24? Between 11 and 11:45 p.m., my aunt Barbara had brought my grandmother home from her house in the village. Also accompanying her were Barbara's daughter, Chari, and her granddaughter, Melanie, just six months old. My aunt got out of the car with my grandmother to help her carry water jugs into the house, when they heard extraordinary vocalizations from only a few feet away.

My grandmother said: "What in the world was that?"

Barbara didn't answer her. She just stood there, in what seemed to be a state of shock, as the screams continued. Her daughter was still in the car with her baby. "Get back in the car, Mom!" she screamed when she heard the noises. And then, in panic, she locked all the doors before her mother could get in the car!

Barbara didn't know what to do. She decided that maybe she'd better go home and get her son Barry and bring him over with his gun. My grandmother, who has a large gun collection, was away camping in the Adirondacks at the time, so there seemed to be no one else to turn to—my father, who lives nearby, was also away.

While Barbara finally managed to get into the car and speed out of the driveway, my grandmother elected for some reason to stay home and protect the house. She was alone there, and that's when she called me. She had armed herself with a hammer.

I must admit that I greeted her call with some skepticism. I was out with friends at a restaurant when I got the call, and I thought that perhaps some animal—a big raccoon, maybe—was making noises outside the house. But when I stopped to think about it, my grandmother had never called me when I was out before to tell me that she was afraid of anything. Once she had singlehandedly chased three men with guns off our property because they were trespassing! So I realized that something was pretty weird. I finished a quick conversation with my friends and bade them goodbye.

My grandmother, meanwhile, was sitting in the house watching all the windows. She was holding her hammer while doing so. She later described the incident:

"When she (Barbara) backed out of the driveway, the thing went down below the hill and it just moaned—oh, the most terrible moan and groan—until the car lights were back in the driveway. Then it came right back up here again and made all these noises again, until he (Barry) got his gun."

When Barry arrived, he heard the screams from just around the house. He fired his shotgun three times to scare off the intruder. Or should I say intruders?

My grandmother added: "I'm sure there were two of them because, by our pine tree out here, there was one making the same noise. Well, when he shot, it just screamed, and this one by the back door, I could see the shadow of this terrible great big thing. Oh, my goodness, that was the worst thing."

"It wasn't until he fired the third time that the thing

screamed and ran off. That time, flame came out of the shotgun."

"Evidently, it (the creature) was there by the air conditioner, probably peeking at me, because the next morning they found imprints where it had been standing underneath the window. It had smashed the grass down and everything."

Well, my skepticism, which had been slowly eroding for the past two years, was now completely shattered. I had never seen three people so frightened or excited as my grandmother, Barry and Barbara. The story really came out of the closet when my mother, who lived less than a mile away and heard the shots that night, wrote a letter to columnist Barney Fowler that was published in the Albany *Times-Union*. The column was headed "Mystery 'Creature' of Kinderhook" and it read, in part:

> No idle talk this; folks in the Town of Kinderhook have been hearing and seeing some strange things. This from a family in the area:
> 'Last Wednesday my mother-in-law, now in her 70s, who lives a quarter-mile up the road from us, came home about 10:30 PM and around the back of the house came this same horrible scream. She was terrified; it screamed, moaned, made guttural noises, and finally my nephew got his shotgun and fired into the air. It moved away, walking on TWO legs, such as a human would do. . . .
> 'Also we have seen some large footprints in the snow, and my husband thought perhaps it might be a bear. . . . Do you or anyone have any idea what this thing could be? On talking to other people in the area, they have heard it too.'

Fowler started up what would become a regular feature of his column for a while when he replied: "I'd be interested in hearing other comments on the creature."

He got them, by the truckload. People wrote in from all around Columbia County relating their experiences. A man from New Lebanon claimed to have heard the same vocalizations "on a foggy, humid night in the woods." Dr. Gary Levine, a paranormal investigator and social sciences professor from nearby Columbia-Greene Community College wrote in to take "a psychic look at the creature." A schoolteacher on Hennett Road claimed to have heard it. There were unverified reported sightings of up to three at once near the Kinderhook Creek the previous year. Tracks were seen and the horrifying vocalizations continued. Fowler's column ran the stories through Halloween, at which point, exasperated, he admitted: "Maybe we've gone overboard on this thing."

Yet, whether they were reported to Barney Fowler or not, sightings and hearings of strange things continued in the Kinderhook area all through 1981, most of which were brought to my attention as the result of a couple of articles I had written on the subject for Albany's *Metroland Magazine* and in Columbia County's *Chatham Courier*. Certainly, no one was in it for the publicity; many eye and ear witnesses preferred to remain anonymous. A perfect example was my own father; I had not heard about his encounter with the creature (or creatures) in his cornfield until I read about it, anonymously submitted, in Fowler's column that busy autumn of 1980.

I went to England that October and, curiously enough, there were many sightings of the infamous "Surrey Puma" at that same time. It seemed as though I couldn't escape alien animals no matter where I went.

Upon my return home I found some interesting things had happened in my absence. In fact, I was beginning to believe that perhaps my absence was required for the creature to show up.

Just before I had returned from abroad in November of that year, Barry and my other cousin, Russell, had been walking up the road toward Cushing's Hill to meet Barry's girlfriend who lived nearby. It was a dark night with a crescent moon. They heard noises—something large and moving—from both sides of the wooded road and momentarily, five figures converged in the middle of the remote road. They were all very tall, and there were no necks apparent beneath their cone-shaped heads. Barry turned around to say something to Russell, but the frightened boy had already taken off down the road.

An interesting corroboration of this sighting was made by Barry's girlfriend, whose name shall remain anonymous. She was coming to meet him from the other direction when she saw an enormous bipedal hairy thing reaching into the garbage can near her house, taking out food and devouring it. She had her small dog with her, and the little pooch was going absolutely bananas. By the time she reached my grandparents' house to meet Barry, she was in a real state of fright; her dog running around in circles, wetting itself and going completely crazy.

After all this activity, I continued my one-man journeys into the wilds of Cushing's Hill, although, I must admit, rarely at night. One would have to more than obsessed to do the equivalent of an Australian walkabout in the dark in an area noted for sinkholes, wild dogs and now, of all things, Sasquatches or something like them.

In February 1981, I was again away in Connecticut when strange footprints appeared on our property. My grandmother told me about it over the phone, and by the time I reached home, the tracks in the snow had partially melted, but they were still very visible. I photographed them on Super 8 movie film, because the oddest thing about these tracks was that they ended dead in the middle of an open field.

The tracks were only about ten inches long, but they were three-toed. They reminded me of the tracks of an enormous duck. They were made by something two-legged. I tried to make casts of them, but the snow prevented them from coming out. While they may have reminded me somewhat of bird tracks, they most emphatically were not. The toes appeared to be pointed and yet very wide; about two inches at the base. Perhaps significantly, we were in the middle of a February thaw on the night the tracks were made.

Just before Easter Sunday of 1981, Barry's girlfriend was riding up Novak Road—one of the hottest spots in Columbia County for creature reports—on her bicycle when this big beast lumbered across the road and into my father's cornfield.

May 8, 1981. My cousin and several friends got another scare in the woods near my father's home. Barry's friends had already set up a campfire down by the creek that borders Cushing's Hill. My cousin arrived a bit late, having just visited his girlfriend again, and he came down the path that leads into the deeper regions of the woods on my father's land. He carried a lantern with him rather than a flashlight. As soon as he got onto the path, he noticed two glowing red eyes, or possibly eyes that reflected in his lantern light. He couldn't say exactly how far off the ground they were, but they were high enough to give him a good case of the creeps.

He proceeded to run rather more quickly down toward the campfire where his friends were gathered. He told them that he'd seen something along the path, and they were not surprised. The four teenage boys told him that "it" had been there ever since they'd had the campsite set up. "Every time we put the fire up," one boy told my cousin, "it will get back a little further away from the fire, and every time the fire starts to die down, it comes in closer and it makes these horrible noises." One of the boys compared the sound to the noise a blade of grass makes when you put it in your mouth and blow on it. A squeaky kind of high-pitched noise, they all agreed.

When my cousin was speaking to the others, "it" was still around. So they kept stoking the fire up and tried to keep "it" away. Finally, after a few rather tense hours, they saw "it," or at least its silhouette, over a ridge. It was tall with long arms and no neck. And it stood erect on two legs. That was at about one a.m. The thing wandered off toward the direction of Cushing's Hill. The boys got no sleep at all that night.

Dr. Gary Levine continued his "psychic" look at the creature that was haunting our area, and concluded that the beast was hanging around us because certain members of my family were psychic. He felt that my grandmother and my cousin Barry were drawing the thing subconsciously. I felt that Levine's tests to determine psychic abilities were rather subjective. He asked my grandmother and my cousin if they had ever had any trouble wearing watches or if they ever knew who was going to call them on the telephone before it rang. They both answered in the affirmative to both questions and Levine determined that they were psychic.

It was Levine's participation in the quest, however, that encouraged the crew from "PM Magazine," the nationally syndicated TV show, to do a segment of the program on what they officially dubbed "The Kinderhook Creature." During the filming, my grandmother thoroughly impressed the show's host, Alan Taffel, who was not at all skeptical after he had spoken to her—or after what happened one night when the crew was setting up their equipment for a taping.

It was in June of 1981, shortly after I had discovered (and made my first plaster cast of) a large three-toed track in the woods near my grandparents' house. The track had been fourteen inches long and seven inches wide in the middle, and looked very strange indeed. The PM crew—and Dr. Levine—were quite impressed with this find, so much so that the crew decided to stay around and shoot a segment that evening in the vicinity of Cushing's Hill.

It happened to be a full moon night. Just as the PM crew was setting up the equipment, just before they turned the sound or cameras on, we all heard three distinct noises coming from the swamp. The first was a monkey chatter, similar to the famous Alan Berry Bigfoot tape from the Pacific Northwest. The second was a really high-pitched scream. The third was more like the infamous "baby crying" sound. Everybody just looked at each other in shocked silence.

Once they got the sound equipment on, they heard nothing more. It was at that time that everyone realized that what had spurred the noises had been the switching on of the big camera lights. In fact, host Alan Taffel, in his original version of his final spiel of the segment, mentioned the noises we had heard, but it was cut from the final show because the producers didn't want to mislead the public.

During the hectic summer of 1981, I was receiving reports from all over the place from people who had seen what they thought was Bigfoot. Most of them were from teenagers or even younger people, and many could be disregarded as misidentification of known animals such as bears (although they're very rare in Columbia County) and even deer. There was one group of people that really impressed me, however. It was a family across the river in the Catskills. They lived at the far end of a dead-end road, bordered on all sides by woods. The husband was a chemist who worked at a laboratory in Albany, and he and his wife and two children were quite terrified by their eerie encounters.

They told me, when I visited them that summer, that they

had had other visitors recently: your basic black, hairy Bigfeet. They said that "it" (or possibly "they") always came out at night, and that their two dogs did not, as a rule, act favorably toward the beasties. They had a huge barrel of fish left outside, and one morning they found the entire barrel had been lifted and put into the woods down by a nearby creek bed. Nearly all of the fish had been taken. They also found some tracks, which they showed me, that were enormous—sixteen inches long. The chemist had shown the tracks to an official at the New York State Department of Environmental Conservation, who remarked: "If those are bear tracks, it's a real monster." To which one might add: if they're not bear tracks, they're made by a monster as well.

Unfortunately, I made the mistake of informing Dr. Levine of the whereabouts of these people, and after his investigation, they refused to come forward with any more information. Apparently, his tactics and attitude, and beliefs that the beings could only be psychic and nothing else, had turned off the people to the whole subject.

August 1981. About 4 a.m. I was awakened from a deep sleep by a noise coming from the woods. When I woke up, I realized I hadn't been dreaming, because I still heard the noise.

What did it sound like? Weird as it sounds, like two enormous monkeys trying to converse with each other. Although I had been watching and listening carefully for months now, and had heard some fairly strange nightbirds and other nocturnal creatures, these were different. I consider this to be the second time I have heard the sound made by the infamous Kinderhook Creature(s).

Being the obsessed maniac that I am, I put my pants on and went outside to look around, but I couldn't find anything that night. In the morning, however, I found an outline of something human-like that had been lying in the tall grass at the edge of the woods, exactly where the noises had seemed to come from. It was an almost fetal-shaped imprint, and when I laid down in it, I discovered that it was about six inches taller than I was—and that was when it was curled up.

On September 8, 1981, a stranger came to my house from

out of the blue. He was a hunter, and he had been out rabbit hunting by Kline Kill Creek, where he had found tracks in the sandbed that amazed him. He had seen us featured on "PM Magazine" he told me, and had asked neighbors where I lived. He insisted I come to look at the tracks. I was expecting to find the usual vague markings, but what I found was something else indeed.

Not only were the tracks fresh and in perfect condition, there were several of them leading into the creek. The loamy soil of the creekbed was perfect for the leaving of footprints, and having convinced myself that the hunter and his wife and children (who were with him) were not perpetrating a hoax, I made plaster casts immediately and had them sent to the New York State Museum and examined by a paleontologist and a physical anthropologist. They couldn't make up their minds about the tracks, and they wouldn't give me an answer in writing. The paleontologist felt they were very strange indeed, and both agreed that: a) they were not fakes, b) they were humanoid but odd, c) they were made by something weighing over 190 pounds. That was a very conservative estimate I felt, because I weigh 190 pounds and my own tracks barely made an imprint into the soil.

By now you're probably saying, "Tracks and noises in the dark are all well and good, but how about more visual sightings?"

There were several. My cousin Chari, who had been in the car on that memorable night of September 24, 1980, saw something strange in my grandparents' driveway in November of 1981. She described it as a "big two-legged thing, reddish-brown, that ran off into the woods" when her car headlights flashed onto it.

A gentleman named Mike Maab, a former employee of the Ichabod Crane School system, was fishing late one afternoon in May of 1982 near a dam not far from Kinderhook. He felt something looking at him, he remarked, and when he looked up, he observed a creature looking at him from across the Kinderhook Creek, perhaps twenty yards off. Maab described the creature as about eight feet tall, with long hair on its head and short hair on its body that was colored a reddish-brown. It had small, beady red eyes and he even noticed that its fingernails were black. After the two had a staring contest for a couple of minutes, the creature ambled off into the woods from where it had apparently come. Maab did not pursue, opting to go home instead.

My third experience with "creature vocalizations" occurred on May 5, 1982, a night I'll never forget for its sheer weirdness. It was at the bridge site at the Kline Kill Creek where the tracks had been found by the hunter.

It was the first night that year I had gone out for an informal check of the area. I had just come from work (Albany), therefore I hadn't stopped at home to pick up a camera or anything. In short, I was woefully unprepared for what happened. I should have known better, because you often seem to have a premonition before this "thing" comes around. It seemed as though there was something mysterious about that whole night.

As I was on my way over to the bridge, some very appropriate things happened. A black cat crossed my path, bats were flying around, frogs were leaping across the road. I mention these oddities only in passing, although the late Charles Fort, well-known for his books on unexplained phenomena and a native of the region, may have been delighted by the atmosphere.

When I finally got to the bridge, I just stopped and parked my car there. I waited for quite a long time, not really expecting to hear anything. After all, it was my first time out there since the fall of 1981.

I decided, after being bored for awhile, to count backwards from one hundred, and if nothing happened by the time I reached one, then I might as well go home. So I began.

When I had counted to fifty or forty-nine, I heard the noises again. They were precisely the same noises that had awakened me the summer before: like the chattering of monkeys, but with tremendous volume as though it came from a very large, or several very large, throats.

I believe that there were two of them there that night, and that they were communicating with each other. It sounded like monkeys trying to articulate, trying almost to imitate human speech, although the sounds themselves could in no way have been made by humans.

I was so surprised that at first I could not move. I had wanted to get out of the car to see what was making the sounds, but my legs would not go. When I finally got up the nerve to get out of the car, I walked across the road to where the sounds had been coming from: a small clump of trees jutting out near a cornfield, perhaps thirty yards away. Now there was no more noise.

But at this point I looked northward. Something had caught my eye. The sky was perfectly clear, and in the northeast, I saw a white light rise up from the horizon. It was just a little ball of light, comparable to the size of a peach held at arm's length. Just a white light, round like a ball. It was going straight up, and it looked as though it had just risen from beyond the trees. It proceeded to ascend in a straight line, far above the horizon.

It seemed to be floating and it made no sound. It wasn't moving very fast: faster than a hot air balloon but slower than an airplane. It reached its zenith in the night sky and then just vanished. I could see it go. Just like a balloon popping (but soundless) as it disappeared. I can truly say, of all the occasions I have hunted for the Kinderhook Creature, I have never been so afraid as I was that night. To be alone in the middle of nowhere and experience the inexplicable is a most unnerving experience. I hastened home in my car.

The next day, however, I went back to the "scene of the crime" and there, indeed, was one of the footprints like I had seen before on the embankment beneath the bridge. I thought it was rather distinct, so I took a picture of it. It was fairly small—only about 12 inches as opposed to the 13¾ inches of the other tracks—but the curious thing was that there was only one, headed in the direction of the water. There was my evidence, circumstantial though it was, that something very odd had passed me the night before in the dark.

I continued to receive unverified reports of Bigfoot sightings from all over Columbia County, but at least one of them is worth mentioning. My aunt owns a seed company in Chatham and it was reported to her by a reliable (but anonymous) witness that two friends of his were hunting near the Berkshires in Austerlitz in the spring of 1982. It was daylight, of course, and somehow the two hunters became separated in the vast woods.

One of them encountered a very tall (about eight feet) red-haired Bigfoot. He was so terrified that he dropped his rifle and ran. The other hunter finally caught up with him and tried to get the frightened man to go back into the woods to retrieve his gun, but he was too afraid to go. The other man had to go and get it for him. "No way could it be a bear," said the hunter who had seen the thing. It had been standing there staring at him, probably wondering what the huge stick was that he was carrying.

If these creatures exist, and if they are biological animals and not some paranormal entities, where could they live and what could they eat? In all my treks up Cushing's Hill, even though I found plenty of dense underbrush, swampland and sinkholes, I never once have been able to locate anything like a real hideaway for a creature to live permanently. The most likely prospect is that the creatures are nomadic, resting wherever they can.

On the other hand, there is a little-explored cave in Red Rock (near Austerlitz) that's about eight miles from my home. It also happens to be an area where a lot of Bigfoot reports have come from. I'm no spelunker, or I would have explored this cave long ago.

In lieu of that, my cohorts and I tried many experiments to get the creature to come to us. I felt that my cousin had made a mistake firing off his gun to scare the things away; they had been making regular nightly visits to our house before, apparently for food they took from the garbage, but now it seemed they were frequenting other areas. We wanted to get them to return.

We modified a birdfeeder on our lawn, took off its sides and placed food on it not meant to attract birds. My cousins and I would leave out large pieces that had gone bad and (cleverly, we thought) would pour flour around the surrounding earth so that whatever took the meat would leave footprints.

We tried different lures, but it always took the steak. When

I say "it" I mean—something took the steak. It obviously had good taste. It wouldn't take hot dogs or chicken, but it would take any kind of steak or beef. But it would never leave footprints. Whatever it was, it was either very cautious not to step in the flour, or it had adequately long arms to reach to steak from a distance.

Once we left an entire box of pizza for the creature. There were only two slices in it, but we left the whole box in the birdfeeder. The next day we found the box down in the bushes at the far end of our property, but the pizza inside hadn't been eaten. Whatever had taken it just left something like claw or fingernail scratches on the box.

Could a dog have been taking the bait? I don't think so. First of all, the birdfeeder is about five feet off the ground. I don't think a dog would jump that high, especially without leaving tracks in the flour.

There is a great deal of evidence (including that found by my father) to suggest that our resident creature eats rabbits— or at least parts of rabbits. We have found bits of rabbits in all the area "hot spots"— but never any blood.

At about the same time we were leaving out the bait, I found an opossum head not far from the birdfeeder. Just the head; I never did find the body. And there wasn't any blood around it either.

During the summer of 1982, my father coincidentally saw something near his birdfeeder around dusk. It was standing out under the large willow tree in his backyard, and he described it (as my grandmother had) as being black. Just a thought: could the creature have deduced that my father would leave out food for them in his birdfeeder, too?

A neighbor who lived up Mill Hill Road (another nearby swampy area) had told me in 1981 of his own experience of hearing vocalizations shortly after he and his family had moved into the area. In 1982, the neighbor, one Philip Winegard by name, also told me that when he was about thirteen and living in Greene County, he had been out hunting birds in a swampy region one day when suddenly a "monkey-like creature about the size of a boy rose up out of the swamp and grabbed a bird in its hands." Winegard did not stay around to get a closer look.

Winegard also told me that in the summer of 1982, a neighbor of his reported that he had found his picnic table torn completely apart one morning. The man said that he had a feeling of "being watched" the night before when he had been outside in his garden. Vandals? Perhaps.

In 1982, during apple season in Kinderhook, there were a number of sightings of a "white Bigfoot" reported. There was also a sighting in the town of Kinderhook itself near an apple orchard. Perhaps significantly, the apples were just ripening at that time of the year. The white "Sasquatch" had been seen running through the apple orchard by a farmer. Perhaps the creature is omnivorous and multi-colored?

There were also several reports of a "white Bigfoot" that winter in the Chatham area. I was keeping the PM Magazine people up to date on the sightings, and when they got in touch with the people in Chatham who had made these reports, they denied ever having made them.

Nevertheless, there were at least three unverified reports of a white Sasquatch or Bigfoot. I checked out the area and found that it was a remote place which had all the trappings of Bigfoot lore. It was near a pond in the woods on an old dead end road. There was only one house on the road. The teenage girl who lived in the house claimed that she had seen this white creature cavorting around in the snow in December of 1982 on at least three occasions. She was really frightened by it. But when the folks from PM called her parents, they just denied the whole thing. The girl herself never denied it, because she wasn't given the opportunity.

My parents' own experience with the "creature" occurred in the early part of 1980, although they wouldn't speak of it until years later. My father had apparently chased the thing through his cornfield one night. He was chopping wood on an early spring evening when he had an eerie sensation he was being watched. Perhaps it was because his tenant, an elderly man who rented the mobile home on my father's land, had recently reported that something had been "pounding his trailer" in the evenings. He had actually called my father over one night to see what it was, but on that occasion he found nothing—

except large footprints in the snow that he took for being those of a bear. Perhaps they were, or . . .

In any case, my father heard a very peculiar noise as he was chopping wood. My mother heard it too, and she compared it to "the sound of a pig being slaughtered." But whatever it was had been in the cornfield. The noises carried on, varying too, including not only the "pig squeal," but "clacking and screeching noises." My father finally tried to pursue the creature into the cornfield, only to hear it seconds later from the other end of the field, about eight acres away! He could never seem to get near it.

What may or may not have been a Bigfoot sighting occurred in September 1983 at about 9 a.m. when an anonymous man (now deceased) saw something on Novak Road, one of the hottest of area "hot spots." The elderly gentleman was driving along and he saw "something" walk out in front of his car and amble across the road and into the swamp. He was so frightened by the encounter that he stopped at a neighbor's house and had the neighbor call us. We tried to get in touch with the man; however, he wouldn't talk about it.

All he told the neighbor was that the animal was "black and big." He varied somewhat on the story when we tried to talk to him. He insisted then that it had merely been a bear. But if it had been, why had he been so terrified that he went into the neighbor's house? And why had he asked the neighbor to call us, knowing our knowledge of Bigfoot? The interesting thing is that he told the neighbor that the creature had walked on two legs—obviously not a bear. As the man died six months later, the secret of what he actually saw died with him.

It was around this time that Walter Brundage came to my door one day. I had never seen the man before in my life, but he had read of our experiences in *The Globe* and had somehow tracked us down. He is from Connecticut and has travelled up and down the east coast researching and investigating Sasquatch sightings. He had some very interesting tales to tell me. Brundage had seen some unusual things in Connecticut. There was a Bigfoot that had been reported to him as walking across a road in front of a car. Brundage went there to check out the area.

On the side of the road, he found a lot of tall grass that had been matted down, and there, he said, you could see the imprint of a body which was very large. You could see where the arm had been curled up around the head, and, as we have seen, our friend does seem to sleep in that position. I thought it was fascinating because that was exactly the kind of imprint I had found in my own woods.

Another interesting anecdote Brundage related was that when he had travelled through Pennsylvania, he found that the theory down there among the locals was the Bigfoot inhabited abandoned mines in the area. I thought that was a very promising idea. Brundage and I have carried on a correspondence since then. It's just one example of how interesting people pop out of the woodwork in their mutual quest for answers.

My parents—and this time my brother and sister as well— were all awakened by weird vocalizations in June 1983 at about 11 p.m. Ironically, I was up at Lake Champlain at the time, helping Saratoga Springs school teacher Joe Zarzynski in his research into reports of the "Champlain Monster."

My family had heard vocalizations—the old "pig slaughter" noise—coming from the woods and garden out in back of the house. No one had nerve enough to actually go outside and see what was making the noises.

About a week later, however, my father discovered what appeared to be a handprint or claw marks etched into the hard wood of his storage shed. The print was about seven feet off the ground. He thought it was a rather disturbing discovery.

In February 1984, my father and uncle were hunting near Cushing's Hill when they found enormous tracks. Although they were brought to my attention a few days later, I didn't get to see them before the snow melted because I had the flu. The lot of a monster hunter seems to be that he's always one step behind the monster.

In any case, the tracks were not only evocative for their size —which my father described as "much larger than his own feet"—but right next to the tracks were the remains of a rabbit. And, once again, there was no blood.

On May 6, 1984—two years and a day after my unnerving

experience at the place I've dubbed "Bigfoot Bridge"—I found three more sets of footprints along the sandbed by the bridge. They were leading into the water on one side of the sandbank and out on the other side. They were made by three different individuals.

There were very tiny tracks, about seven inches long (baby Bigfoot?), along with a middle-size one, which was the only one I successfully cast in plaster, some 10½ inches long. The big one was 13¾ inches. They were extremely fresh, and like all the other tracks I had discovered there, they had five toes.

Later that same month, my cousin Barry, ever on the lookout, heard more weird vocalizations near the apple orchards in Kinderhook. He didn't see anything, though, and my impression is that he didn't look very hard. The whole subject is a bit close to him at this point, and it frightens him more than he cares to admit.

My brother and sister, who are both in their late twenties, were walking on Novak Road near Cushing's Hill on the night of May 18, 1984 when they too heard frightening vocalizations emanating from the mist-enshrouded swamp. My brother remains a skeptic, but my sister believes there is something there.

One of the oddest vocalizations heard by us occurred on June 1, 1984 at around 1:30 a.m. My grandmother woke me up to tell me that she heard "a laughing cry, like a laughing hyena" from not far outside her window. I got up and dressed quickly, and as I was dressing, I heard the noises myself. I grabbed my tape recorder and switched in on—and of course, the noises ceased. But we heard the vocalizations a total of about six times.

On June 13, Philip Winegard reported to me that his neighbor—the same unfortunate soul who had his picnic table torn apart a couple years previously—had been awakened by "heavy breathing" outside his window. His wife urged him to see what was making the noise, but he refused to go outside. The two of them heard loud vocalizations which seemed to trail off into the swampy area behind their home. Needless, to say, they didn't get much sleep the rest of the night.

All the reports of vocalizations reminded me of an experience I had as a child. There had been another entity reputed to haunt our woods then, and if Kinderhook is indeed a haunted place, I wondered what the connection between Bigfoot and what we used to call "the white blob" could have been?

When I was ten years old (1962), I was up in the woods behind our house with my cousin Chari, who was then age seven. We both heard this really high-pitched whistle noise, and I turned and looked in the direction of the sound. There was a white object peering at me from behind a nearby pine tree. I say "peering," but in fact it had no eyes that I could discern. It looked like a big amorphous blob and it really scared the bejesus out of me. My cousin and I took off down the hill at an enormous speed. The thing that strikes me odd about this encounter—aside from the obvious—is that the noise the "blob" made is very similar to the noises often attributed to Bigfoot. I don't know what it means; I don't pretend to have any explanation for the similarities.

Explanations aside, the "blob" seemed to periodically pop up in our woodlands. Two years later, just before my twelfth birthday, a friend of mine had been walking through the woods alone when he came running into the house. He told me, breathlessly, that he had just seen this "big white blob" gliding down the hill toward him. It had scared him so much that he jumped over a pond that's about six feet wide; his terrified feet just sailed right over it.

At first I thought he was just joking around, but then I got to thinking that I had seen the same thing two years before—and I had never told him of it for fear of what he'd think of me. So the two of us, pitchfork and shovel in hand as weapons, went into the woods to look for the thing.

We saw something—or it saw us. In broad daylight. My friend stopped on the trail suddenly, his face as white as a sheet, and pointed straight ahead without saying a word. I saw a large white shape that seemed to hover in the trees. We had been all set to "murder" the thing with our weapons, but when we saw that, we dropped our shovel and pitchfork and ran.

It just gets more and more strange. I never told my cousins, Barry and Russell, about the entity either, but when they were about fourteen, Barry reported seeing something along the same lines as me. He and Russell had been down at the lean-to that they had built in the woods when they had seen a "white, almost bell-shaped kind of thing" glide down the hill toward them. Russell had seen it too—but he described it as "looking like the Virgin Mary." This really takes us into some strange territory. What possible connection could there be between Bigfoot and an apparition.

It always amuses me when a former skeptic becomes converted. While all of this has been going on, my grandfather has insisted there must be "a logical explanation." But one night in 1981, he had an encounter of his own. He had a tent set up in the woods on our land, and there was something outside it one night that really shook him up. It was very large, and it shook him up so much that he reached for the gun beneath his sleeping bag. Whatever the thing was, he could see it silhouetted through his tent. It was rifling through the clothes that he had outside. And he insisted that it walked on two legs. The next morning when he came into the house, he was still terrified. Of course, if you ask my grandfather about it now, he'll smile and say it was just a bear. But we've heard that one before.

I've been saving my own sighting of "something" for last. In November 1980, shortly after I had returned from England, my cousin Barry, his girlfriend, and my cousin Russell were all strolling outside during the evening. Suddenly, we heard something large moving through the bushes in the field and Barry ran off in front of everybody else and started chasing whatever moved there.

He pursued it out into the field and we all followed. And that was the night I think I saw something.

I'm not really sure. Maybe it was a reflection of something, or maybe it was my mind playing tricks on me. But Barry was staring at a certain spot in the forest. He could see the thing better than any of us because he was closer. He seemed transfixed, "almost in a trance," as he told me later.

But when I looked to where his eyes were focused, I could see what looked to me like two reddish eyes. They were about six feet off the ground. That was all I saw, for in a moment they had disappeared into the night. But they were there (or seemingly there) long enough to give me a sense that we were in the presence of something quite unknown. The creature, if that's what it was, just seemed to vanish after that, and we left the scene shortly thereafter.

The final episode in this chapter is a transcript of a "creature" sighting that gives one an idea of just how bizarre and paranormal most of the Kinderhook sightings have been. The witness is a highly credible woman, a housewife and mother and a friend of mine for many years. Bob Bartholomew and I both interviewed her on separate occasions, and her story never varied in one detail. I am convinced she saw something. What was it? Perhaps the reader can decide.

Interview with Margaret Mayer on her creature sighting. Questions asked by Bob Bartholomew and Bruce Hallenbeck at Mrs. Mayer's home on June 15, 1985.

BB. Could you describe the time you saw this?

MM. It was about 11 p.m. . . . or 11:10, Friday, June 14. It was a clear night; there was no moon. I was going about fifty miles an hour on Rt. 203 near the Winding Brook Golf Course. It [the creature] was on the left-hand side of the road. The first thing I noticed was the eyes. I sort of thought it was a deer. The eyes were down almost level with the road at first. Then it sort of slid up to the top of the road. It didn't really look like it walked. It was like four or five feet taller than when I first saw it. It stood there for a little while, and it looked across the road, looked in my direction. . . . It blinked while it was looking at me. Then it crossed the road, and by then I was almost to the bottom of the hill. It just seemed to all of a sudden appear on the other side of the road. But the shoulders and the head were like way in front of the legs. I really didn't see the bottom of the legs.

BB: So you saw what would be the shoulders on a human being?

MM: That's right. It would have been about the shoulders up mostly. A little below the shoulders. The head was really way out in front of the legs.

BB: Almost like a bird.

MM: Yeah, sort of. In that position. But that's the odd thing. When I think of it, it seemed to crouch, and when it moved, it didn't straighten up or anything like that. And it moved fast without any awkward movement for something that big.

BB: When you say it moved, did it walk?

MM: When it moved . . . I don't know if I can describe the way . . . at first . . . even with the road. Then it was like something going from being level with the road to being . . . five feet taller. I think it was either sitting on the side of the road or . . . I can't really say what happened. But then it seemed to be at least six or seven feet tall when it rose to its full height. It wasn't a person. There was quite an amount of space from the top of the head to the shoulders.

BB: Much bigger than a person's?

MM: Oh, yes. The eyes were sort of small—not really big—but very far apart. It looked straight at me a couple of times. It only moved from the top part of its shoulders and the head. I didn't notice any arms. I could see the top of the legs, but the odd thing is they were really skinny . . . either skinny or huddled, or else it didn't have arms. It looked . . . deformed. That's why I was surprised it could move so fast. It didn't walk across the road. It stood there for a little while . . . and the hill isn't that long. I didn't really see it move, but all of a sudden it was on the other side of the road. I think it was sort of light-colored, because I could barely see its outline . . .

BB: You say it went across the road but it didn't really walk. You said before it might have floated . . .

MM: Well, it seemed to float up from where it was. Like I said, maybe it had been sitting down. It went from something either lying or sitting by the side of the road to standing up . . . then it started to move . . . and it was on the other side of the road. It didn't seem to walk across the road. It seemed a smoother type of movement . . . almost gliding . . . it didn't have enough time to just walk. . . . It seemed as though it was thinking, "Should I stay here or should I cross the road?" It didn't seem surprised to see me. It wasn't afraid. It was like, "Do I have time to cross the road?"

BB: Did you notice any sign of intelligence?

MM: Oh, definitely . . . it seemed to be thinking. Whether it was about crossing the road or what, I don't know. But obviously, just the way it looked at me, and then it looked across the road. But . . . it wasn't startled. It seemed to be used to the surroundings.

BH: Did you notice ears, a nose or mouth?

MM: . . . I don't know if it was a mouth or a chin. There was some kind of indentation on the bottom of the face. The eyes were really far apart . . . almost to the side of the head. The face seemed flat. It didn't seem to have a nose. . . . It scared me. Not that I didn't think it was strange all along, but then it appeared on the other side of the road and was gone. It bothered me a lot. I rushed home to get my husband and I couldn't find him . . . that was awful.

BB: So, here's this thing near the ground, and all of a sudden it rises up and it turns, blinks . . .

MM: And it turned again . . . and then it seemed to appear on the other side of the road . . . just the way it looked at me—that sort of got me. I was . . . surprised.

BH: Did you notice any odor?

MM: No.

BB: Any noises?

MM: I think it was . . . quiet . . . it's really strange. It's such a busy road and cars are usually travelling . . . and there wasn't anybody.

. . . It seemed to be thinking. Whether it was about crossing the road or what I don't know. Just the way it looked at me . . . it seemed used to the surroundings. But, I've been interested in the Yeti, but I always thought it was an ape-like thing. But this—sometimes I almost think it flew across the road. Not that I saw it fly . . . it's such an odd shape. And when it moved . . . it didn't move the whole body. Just the top part and the head. It didn't move its bottom half. Maybe it didn't have one.

[The eyes were yellow] . . . and the head went right into the shoulders of the body—no neck.

The Skene Valley Country Club of Whitehall, New York where creatures have been seen and heard over the years.

Photo by Bill Brann

Plaster casting made by Bill Brann of a track found on March 3, 1977 at Pine Lake, northwest of Whitehall, New York.

Sketch of the creature sighted along Abair Road, rural Whitehall, New York in August of 1976.

Drawing by Eric Miner

Drawing by Eric Miner

The artist's impression of Bigfoot based on various eyewitness descriptions.

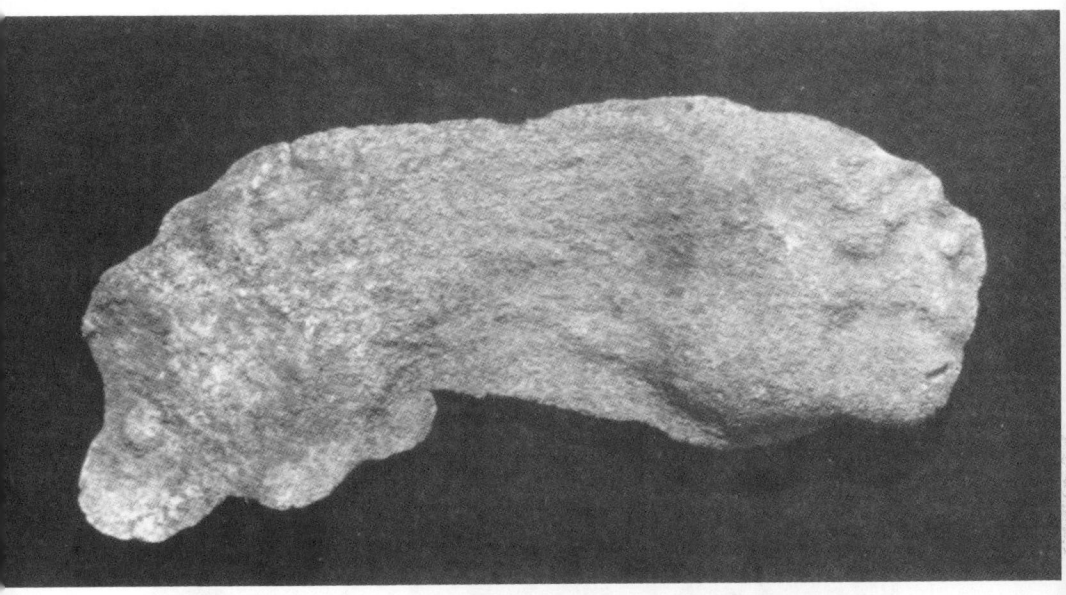

Photo by Bill Brann

A small casting of a footprint found in Kinderhook in 1983, displaying the characteristic curvature. Measuring only 9½ inches, this may be evidence of a small breeding pool in the area.

Photo by Jeff and Ted Pratt

This photograph of a hulking form, which some have suggested is a Bigfoot creature, was taken in rural Chittenden, Vermont in 1976. Laboratory analysis of the negative proved inconclusive, while an expedition to the site found no plausible explanation for the image.

A close-up of the mysterious Bigfoot creature.

Sketch by Rob DuBois

Artist's rendition of Sparks creature as it appeared in Adirondack Bits'n Pieces.

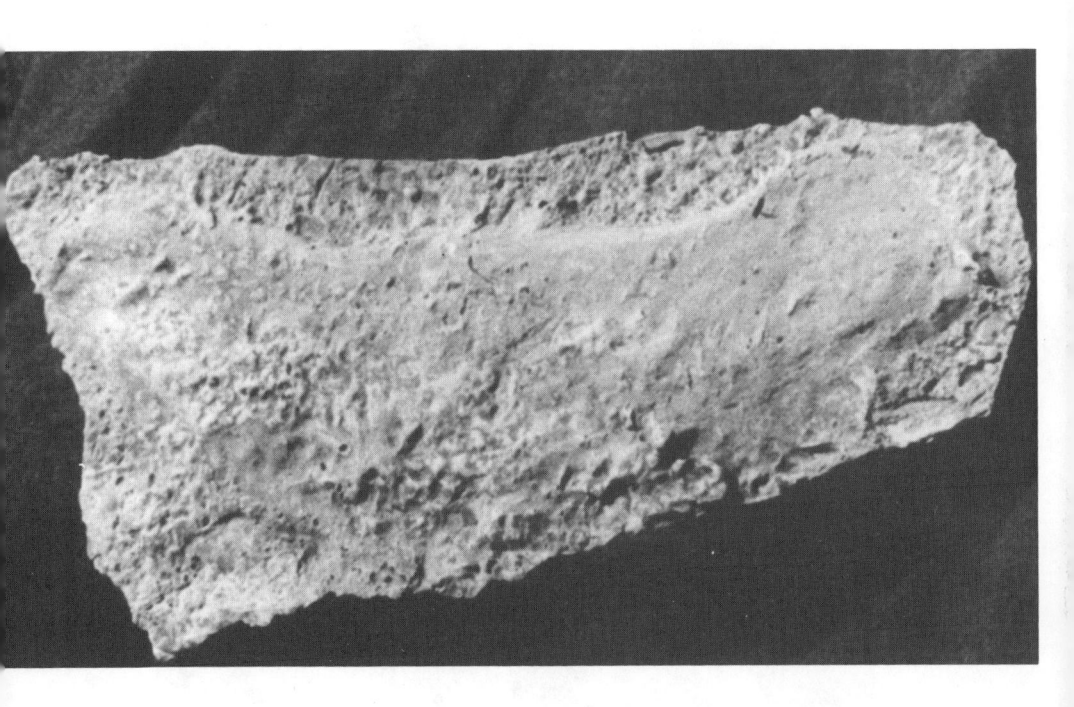

Photo by Clifford South

Plaster casting of 19½-inch footprint by a deputy sheriff in the fall of 1976 along the Poultney River.

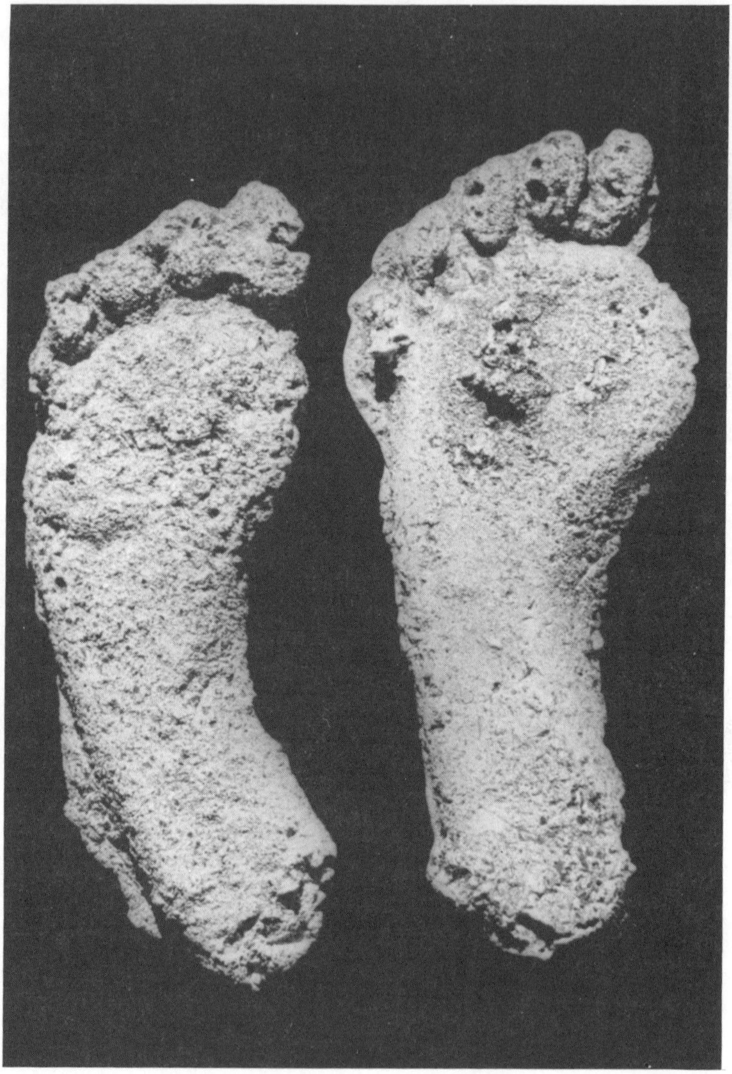

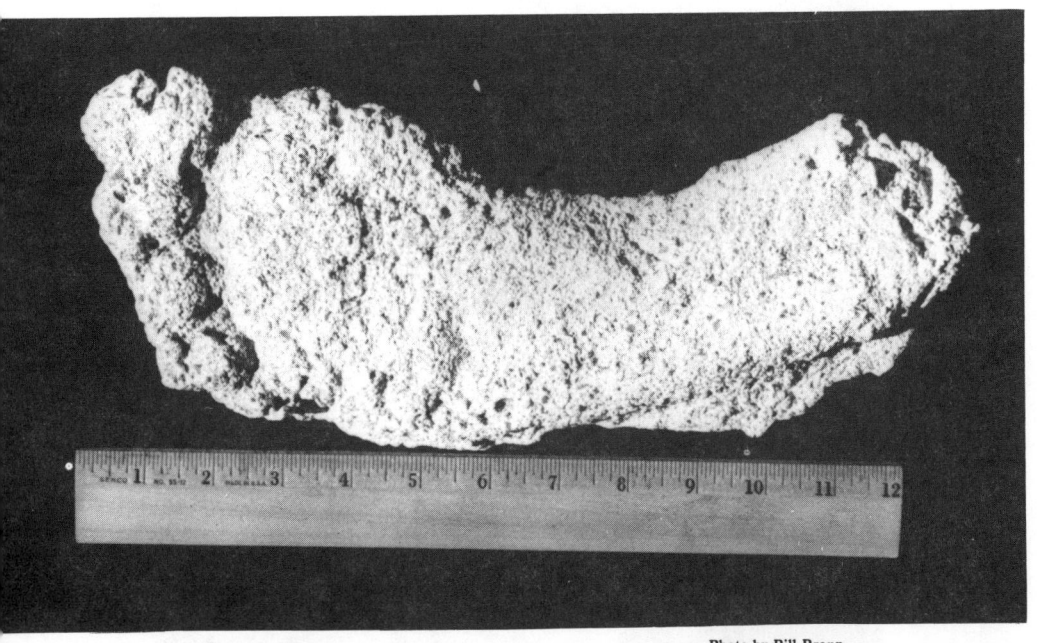

Photo by Bill Brann

Plaster castings of footprints measuring over 13 inches found at Kline Kill Creek, Kinderhook, New York on September 8, 1981.

Plaster casting of a footprint found on a logging road in West Rutland, Vermont on September 20, 1985.

Dr. Warren Cook and his daughter, Susan, encountered a Bigfoot while driving along Rt. 4A through West Rutland, Vermont.

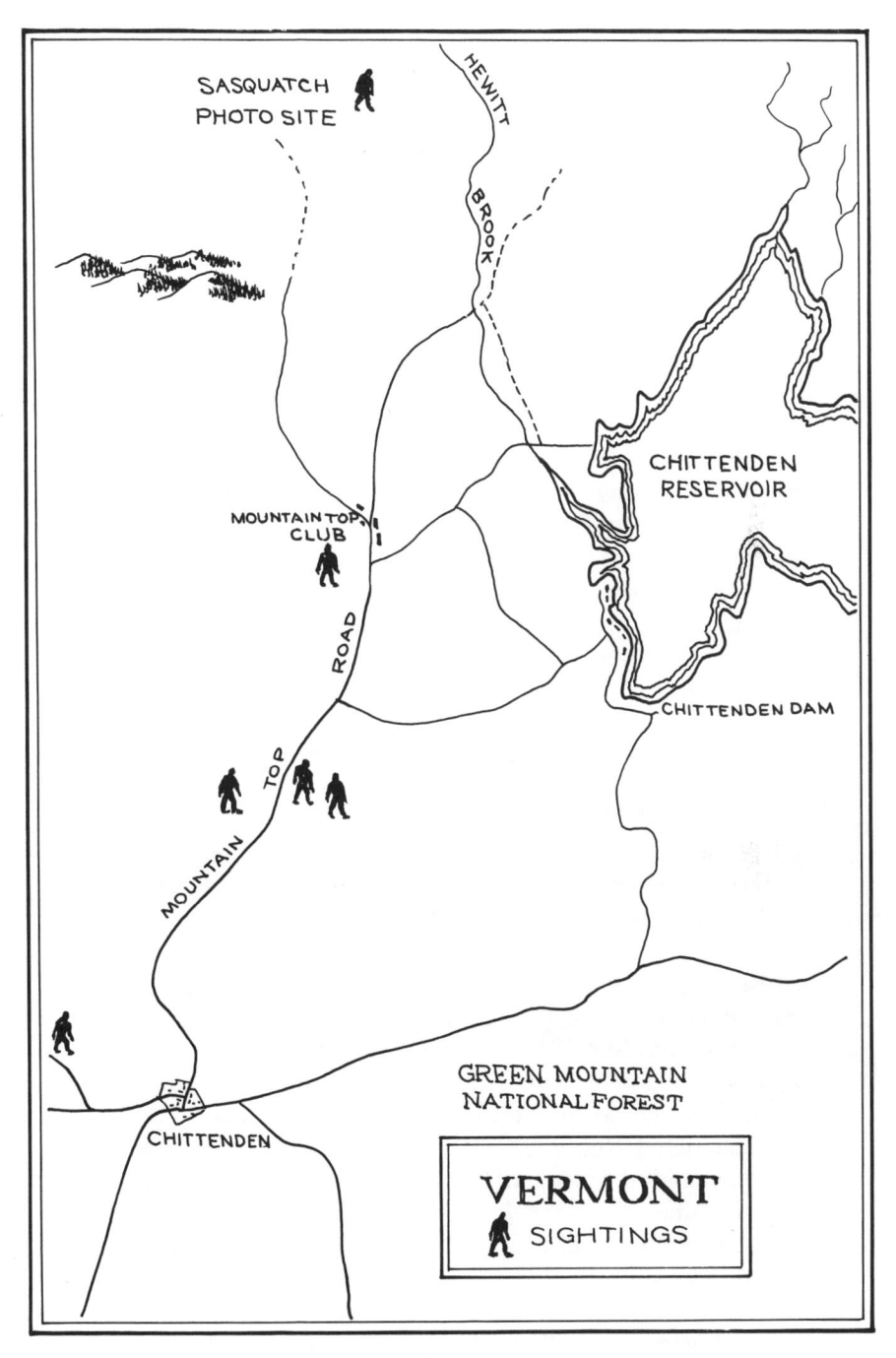

Sighting locations in Vermont. Figure at top of map is the location where the first Vermont Sasquatch was accidentally photographed.

Chapter 6

THE UFO ANGLE

At first glance, UFOs and Bigfoot reports appear unrelated, other than being unexplained phenomena. Yet, there are about one hundred cases from around the world of Bigfoot-type creatures spotted simultaneously in the vicinity of UFOs,[1] or within a few hours before or after.[2] Large hairy ape-like creatures have also been reported coming to and from UFOs, with some alleged contact witnesses claiming they observed Bigfoot-like creatures inside such ships, usually along with small humanoids. Bigfoot has also been seen engulfed in a bright light. When you first consider the relationship between UFOs and Bigfoot the link sounds silly and far-out. Bigfoot an extraterrestrial? It would be tempting to sweep these reports under the rug or dismiss them as wild imagination. Yet, this pattern has been noted by other researchers, and the pattern holds true with Bigfoot sightings in New York and Vermont.

During the 1976 Whitehall Bigfoot wave, UFOs were seen across New York State, with dozens of reports coming from Whitehall itself. One particular case in late August involved a woman who called Whitehall Police to say that a UFO had landed in a small field near her house along Second and Vaughn Streets at about 10 p.m. Sergeant Wilfred Gosselin and dispatcher Robert Martell responded, and upon arriving at the site found a circular patch of matted grass about twenty feet in diameter. Strangely, Martell later said, "It was warm, as if it were giving off heat."[3]

The same night as officer Brian Gosselin's Bigfoot encounter at around midnight on August 25, a nearby Smith Road resident reported a UFO to the Washington County Sheriff's

Department. In fact, "bright lights" strange enough to prompt calls to local law enforcement agencies were logged by several Whitehallers that night. Neighboring towns also experienced the phenomenon.[4]

At about eight p.m., two brothers from bordering Low Hampton observed a slowly moving "great big light" over Leonard's Apple Orchard, which they said was "too low" and "too bright" to be a star.[5] Later a Granville resident claimed to see an unidentified "greenish light" in the sky. As the evening progressed, other reports flowed into Warren and Washington County police agencies. Alerted to the reports, Walter Kruger, a Washington County Deputy Sheriff observed a "large light moving slowly in the north." A second deputy, along with a conservation officer also reported strange aerial lights.[6]

It was also on August 25 that three Yonkers residents about two hundred miles south of Whitehall, Marie Diguardia, and Delia and Deborah Debanedetto, were driving along the Westchester side of the Tappan Zee Bridge at about 8:05 p.m. when they sighted a silver-colored object. Meantime, an Elmsford resident, Kathlene Vasinsac, said that several motorists pulled over near the bridge on Rt. 9 to watch a large saucer-shaped object visible for some ten minutes. It hovered, then "slowly ascended at an angle and headed east."[7]

At about the same time, Richard Cross, his son, along with Daniel Ambrose and his daughter observed a strange UFO over Pomona, New York.[8] In fact, scores of mystified residents of Rockland County reported seeing UFOs of various colors between August 20 and 25.[9]

Just prior to the Bigfoot flap, the UFO wave had begun. John Wallace Spener, in *The UFO Yearbook* (1976, p. 87) noted that back on August 20, four days before the Abair Road incident, two police officers from nearby Greenwich, Hubert Salamon and Edward McGinty, watched with Christopher Knight of Glenville as an unusual aerial light changed from red to green to white.

Just after midnight on August 22, Mr. and Mrs. Gus Bizas, and Police Officer William Patrick watched with curiosity as a mysterious object hovered over the Orange and Rockland Lovett Power Plant at Tompkins Cove. "[It was] like a ball of fire, but not red or orange, more like the color of a light bulb, very, very bright," said Patrick.[10]

At about 10 p.m. two days later, Robert Stuber, his wife, daughter and Officer Patrick, all witnessed an unusual aerial light change from red to green and later white. During the five-day wave, Patrick recorded five separate sightings.[11] Over a three-week period in August, upwards of one hundred UFO reports were documented in Rockland and Putnam Counties alone.

Three other UFO-Bigfoot reports have been recorded in New York State. In autumn 1967 there were hearsay reports of a large hairy creature in an area near Ithaca, during a major UFO wave. One story alleges that a group of teens searching the woods came across a creature which tore one of the boys' jackets.[12]

Between 1966-1969 many neckers parking at Mount Misery in Huntington, Long Island claim to have been startled by a seven-foot tall human-like creature. The periodic reports turned up where many low-flying cigar and saucer-shaped objects were seen.[13]

During late 1974 and lasting into early 1975, large hairy creatures, walking upright, were observed crossing roads and wandering in wooded sections of Staten Island. Sightings correspond with UFO reports in the area.[14]

UFO-Bigfoot correlations continued into the 1980s. On April 10, 1980, five New Windsor, New York children, ranging from eight to fifteen, observed a diamond-shaped object engulfing the area "in every color of the rainbow." It was seen hovering over nearby swampland and woods. After two days of searching the swamps for possible leads, a large, flat, dry area was found with four-toed prints measuring 18½ inches along the outside of a dry spot.[15]

On the evening of May 5, 1982, Kinderhook, New York native Bruce Hallenbeck was staking out an active Bigfoot site when he encountered something quite odd:

> I saw something and I heard something. . . . I went to the same place where tracks were found and just turned off my car and sat there in the dark. . . . The first thing that happened was I saw a white light go up in the sky,

from it seemed like somewhere out in the field, but it was probably farther away. It was a white ball . . . making no sound whatsoever. It seemed to go pop (not audibly) and disappeared. And almost a second after that, I heard these really strange noises almost next to me in the woods, just a few yards away . . . I can only describe them as something like two big monkeys trying to communicate with each other . . . yacking back and forth. And I tried to get up to get out to see what it was, but my legs wouldn't cooperate. I was a little too scared. . . . By the time I did manage to move out of the car and toward the woods, whatever it was had stopped making the noise. At that point I was scared enough so I left anyway.[16]

Sightings in Vermont have also exhibited this unusual pattern. The September 29, 1985 edition of *The Sunday Rutland Herald and The Sunday Times Argus* featured an article on Rutland UFO investigator William Chapleau. He is the Vermont State director of the Mutual UFO Network, a civilian UFO study group. In a lengthy article by Monica Allen entitled "For UFO Hunter, Seeing is Believing," Chapleau mentions a possible UFO-Bigfoot connection in the West Rutland case of September 20:

> There have been recent sightings in the Rutland area over the Rutland Country Club, according to Chapleau. In fact, people began calling in to report a strange lighted object in the area last week.
> Around the same time, a group of West Rutland people saw a large creature on a gravel road near Route 4A in West Rutland. Castleton State College Anthropologist, Dr. Warren Cook, a specialist on the legendary creature known as Bigfoot, took castings of the footprints which measured 14 inches long.
> Chapleau said there have often been sightings of Bigfoots—also known as Sasquatches—around the same time as UFOs are sighted. He theorizes these creatures may be left by beings from another world for testing purposes, as humans might leave a monkey.
> Chapleau admits he has "an active imagination" that's gotten more active as he's read hundreds of books on UFOs.

Chapleau adds that shortly after these creature encounters, he found an "oval-shaped patch" of dried and discolored ferns measuring about thirty-three feet by sixteen feet, within a mile of where the sightings took place. He noted that a small birch tree was bent over at an angle to the patch and that four eight-inch or ten-inch square patches were found as well. Chapleau pondered whether this was where a UFO may have temporarily set down.[17]

Perhaps Dr. Warren Cook best summarized the feelings of many researchers when he commented on the possible UFO-Bigfoot link:

> Over the years, I've been aware that that is the case and it surpasses my understanding. I haven't been able to draw any conclusions one way or another. The data ... that's the way it occurred. Those coincidences have occurred, whether they are just coincidences or whether there is a connection, I don't know.[18]

Do Bigfeet and UFO sightings happening around the same time in the same vicinity indicate some sort of coincidence? Or is it possible that the same social conditions or "mind set" that make a group ripe for a UFO wave also predispose them to other supernatural events like Bigfoot? These are some of the theories we will examine in Chapter 8 as we try to come to some conclusion as to what's really going on.

References:

1. Moravec, Mark, *the UFO-Anthropoid Catalogue: Cases Linking Unidentified Flying Objects and Giant Anthropoid Creatures.* Published by the Australian Centre for UFO Studies, November 1980.
2. Approximately 40 cases of UFO-Bigfoot cases were collected from various UFO specialty journals by Bob Bartholomew while he was working for Robert C. Girard's Arcturus Book Service, Scotia, NY between 1983 and 1985. The Bookstore specializes in UFO-related materials, and has since relocated to Stone Mountain, GA.
3. Personal interview by Paul Bartholomew with Whitehall Police Dispatcher, Robert Martell.

4. Gilbert, Allen, "Hairy Monsters Or Little Green Men? Whitehall Folk Aim To Find Out Which," *Rutland Daily Herald* (Vermont), August 27, 1976.
5. Report by Marie Rice of Newswatch 13, late August 1976 on WAST-TV, Channel 13, Menands, NY
6. Gilbert, Allen, "Hairy Monsters Or Little Green Men? Whitehall Folk Aim To Find Out Which," *Rutland Daily Herald* (Vermont), August 27, 1976.
7. Spencer, John W., *The UFO Yearbook*. Springfield, MA: Phillips, 1976, p. 91.
8. Ibid., p. 92.
9. Ibid., p. 92.
10. Ibid., p. 88.
11. Ibid., p. 90.
12. Moravec, Mark, *The UFO-Anthropoid Catalogue: Cases Linking Unidentified Flying Objects and Giant Anthropoid Creatures*. Published by the Australian Centre for UFO Studies, November 1980, p. 16.
13. Ibid., p. 16.
14. Ibid., p. 29.
15. "Six Close Encounters Wreak Terror in 40-Mile UFO Corridor," *Star*, August 3, 1982. Despite sensational treatment given these cases by this newspaper, the reports are apparently based on true incidents.
16. From "Bigfoot in the Northeast," a 1989 audio documentary produced and narrated by Paul Bartholomew.
17. From a telephone interview between Paul Bartholomew and William Chapleau, November 16, 1991.
18. From "Bigfoot in the Northeast," (1989), audio documentary produced and narrated by Paul Bartholomew.

Chapter 7

VERMONT ENCOUNTERS

A boy stands on the platform of a country railway station. As the trains come and go, he notes their numbers in his notebook, along with their times of arrival and departure. And one day, reviewing his notes, he discerns a pattern; there are recurrences, frequencies, periodicities. And gradually he senses, beyond the isolated events he has been noting, the larger process. . . .

—Hilary Evans*

Encounters with large, hairy two-legged creatures across what is now the state of Vermont were commonly described among the Indians and early European settlers. In modern times, sightings of creatures fitting virtually the same description continue to be reported with increasing frequency.

The history of 20th century Bigfoot reports in the rolling Green Mountains of Vermont began in 1951. During a cold February day in the dead of winter, lumberman John Rowell and a man named Kennedy were in the town of Sudbury, snaking hardwood logs from Sudbury Swamp. The desolate swamp is south of Middlebury, between Otter Creek and Rt. 22. The previous night, they had left an oil drum weighing several hundred pounds on a tractor seat. The drum was covered with canvass. The next morning they were startled to find the drum carried toward the woods several hundred feet. Around the tractor was an eerie sight: dozens of huge, naked footprints.

Rowell hurried to Middlebury and purchased film for his

Polaroid camera and when he returned snapped several photos. He gave them to a Middlebury newspaper in hopes that one would be published, but none appeared. The impressions measured twenty inches long and eight inches wide at the toes, which were turned straight down. Rowell estimated the fuel drum weighed 450 pounds.[1]

During 1961 or 1962, farmer William Lyford of Plainfield heard his normally content cows making a commotion one night at Lanesboro Station, on the Well River-Barre Railroad. Upon investigating, he observed a tall, hairy creature, which he said couldn't have been a bear because of its upright position. When he shone his flashlight at it, the figure turned and ran, vanishing over a hill and into the darkness.[2]

A group of at least six people, including John Rose of Castleton Corners, spotted the creature either during 1964 or 1965, in the town of Stockbridge, Rutland County while riding in a pick-up truck at about 7:30 p.m. They were on a rural stretch of road when suddenly a seven to eight-foot-tall grayish-colored creature came striding across the road within twenty feet of the vehicle. The sighting didn't last long, as the figure walked briskly. Rose had a good look in the clear moonlit night:

> ... what I saw now was a thing to the right of us, about fifteen - twenty feet ahead, come out of the bushes and just make one leap across the road, and it was gone. It was on two legs ... one stride ... like when you're going to cross a little stream, you push off and you land with your foot out in front of you ... just like one stride.[3]

The year 1974 yielded a pair of eyewitness encounters. In the third week of March, two young men were driving along Country Club Road in Barre, Vermont, when they pulled over to go to the bathroom. They were suddenly startled by a loud "shriek."

"We both looked toward the direction from which the shriek came. We could see a tall, dark figure running across a field that had a dusting of snow. What amazed me was the speed at which this creature could run and at the length of its arms ... hands swung below the knees as it ran," the pair wrote in a letter to Dr. Warren Cook.

The next recorded incident occurred in 1974, near Rutland and is admittedly vague. It involved a couple that reportedly saw an eight to ten-foot monster covered with hair, in a meadow some time after midnight. Police examining the area said the creature ran across the road in front of them. Beyond this, little is known.[4]

In late August or early September 1975, a man, his brother and son were resting on a hilltop adjacent to Missisquoi Bay (Vermont side of Lake Champlain) when they glimpsed a large hulking figure. The account was relayed in a letter to Dr. Cook:

> It as far from a 'close encounter' (an estimated distance, as the crow flies, of about a mile and a half). I distinctly recall my brother exclaiming 'What the hell was that?' We all watched the creature for a period of several minutes, walking at a casual pace along a tractor-trail. . . . How tall would be difficult to guess (possibly eight feet) . . . It was dark in color . . . long in the legs, Wide in the shoulder. Comfortably upright—gait leisurely. It seemed to be in slow-motion and yet it covered a large distance in a few minutes. Ultimately, it turned left and disappeared in the woods.

Rutland County was also the scene of the only known photograph of a possible Vermont Bigfoot. During October, a well-known Rutland County businessman, who for business reasons prefers his name withheld, snapped a picture of a double-log bridge transversing a small stream in a remote section of Chittenden. He took the photo to show a National Forest official the minimal effect of the bridge on the environment. When the picture was developed, he was surprised to see what appeared to be a huge Bigfoot-like creature (upper torso and head) apparently watching him. Castleton State College Anthropologist Warren Cook sent the original negative to a California lab for analysis, which turned up nothing suspicious in terms of negative tampering. On the other hand, dark areas where the face would be did not reveal any facial features.[5]

Barring some unusual photographic quirk, which was ruled

out by the California lab, and barring the possibility of a hoax, which also appears unlikely, Dr. Cook hypothesized what seemed the only other possible natural explanation; perhaps the man took a photo of a large tree stump which had since been removed. Cook discarded this theory when an examination of the area turned up no trace of a stump or stump hole.

The next incident reportedly occurred in north-central Vermont during late 1976 or early 1977. A student of Dr. Cook at Castleton College related that a friend claimed to have observed a pair of Bigfoot creatures running alongside his moving car. Unfortunately, Cook was unable to contact the original witness; thus, nothing more is known.[6]

In March of 1977, in Chittenden, Rutland County, a housewife, who wishes to remain anonymous, looked out her living room window and saw a hairy, ape-like creature standing in a nearby sloping field. She was emphatic that the figure was not a bear. It slouched with its arms hung by its sides, while it stared toward the horizon. Frantically she phoned her husband who was nearby. Although he raced out the back door and grabbed his gun, it was already gone.[7] What "it" was remains a mystery.

During July or August 1977, Rutland County was again the site of an unusual creature report. While returning from roller skating one night at about 10:15, James and Nancy Ingalls encountered something where old Rt. 7 rejoins new Rt. 7, south of the junction with Rt. 103 in Clarendon. The creature was man-like with eyes that glowed red in the headlights. They estimated its height as 6½ feet. The next day, Mr. Ingalls returned to the spot and found large tracks resembling naked human feet, measuring fourteen to sixteen inches long and five inches wide.[8]

In the Rutland area between 1976 and 1978, there was a second-hand account of two couples seeing a Bigfoot from their car. It reportedly walked over a barbed-wire fence.[9] One of the couples also said it found footprints near a swimming area.[10]

On November 28 of 1978, Mr. and Mrs. David Fretz, formerly of the city of Rutland, were just getting accustomed to their new life in the country, having recently moved to nearby

Shrewsbury. On the 27th, a two-inch snowfall—the first real sticking accumulation of the season—blanketed the area around their home on Upper Cold River Road. Mrs. Fretz got home on the 28th at the usual time, roughly 4:45 p.m., from her job as a Rutland school teacher. Husband David picked up the story:

> ... she was getting ready to prepare dinner by going out and picking some Brussel sprouts out of the garden ... she and our little dog and our stepson Scott [French] went out to the garden. Carrying a flashlight on the way back they noticed that the dog started growling and smelling the ground very much up and down a line. When they turned the flashlight on the ground, they saw these rather large footsteps about ... I measured them the next day—they're six inches across, 4 inches deep, about fourteen inches long.[11]

David, who snapped a whole roll of film on the strange prints, said his first reaction was "who of our friends in the city wanted to give us a bit of a scare by coming out here and putting footprints all around the house?" The prints circled around their house after coming off the town road. David continued:

> It was very obvious that somebody had gotten out on one side of our house, the town road, and put on their nice, big fake feet and then walked around our house, back onto the town road, taken their feet off, then driven away. At least that's what everybody thought was our best explanation ... The prints were very, very distinct, all about the same—all very heavy in the snow ... and the toes ... five toes on each foot.[12]

Fretz was confident that soon someone would arrive and tell him it was all a joke, but no one has yet. A game warden examined the area at the request of Fretz and only would say the three-foot strides hadn't been made by a bear.[13]

Dr. Cook believed it significant that the Fretzs' did not seek publicity from the case. Despite concern over finding the huge prints, they did not call police. Cook learned of the case through Scott French, their stepson, who was a student in Cook's class at Castleton College.

During November 1978, about the time of the Fretz incident, northern Vermont was the scene of "Goonyak" reports. As the story goes, a farmer in the area supposedly shot the creature—a hulking, two-legged, eight-foot giant—in the Craftsbury-Morrisville region. He reportedly shot the monster after it broke into his barn, dragging his 1,000-pound Holstein bull 500 yards into an open field. The creature took "ten shots in the chest with a 30.06 rifle" until it died.[14]

The fantastic story grew even more unbelievable, as it was said the creature was then taken under armed guard to a secret location on the fourth floor of the building at the University of Vermont and autopsied. A newspaper reporter from the *Rutland Herald*, Kevin Duffy, heard the Goonyak rumors and decided to call the University. He wrote:

> A check on such an autopsy with Chief Medical Examiner Dr. Eleanor McQuillen and professors of animal pathology, zoology and botany at the University of Vermont resulted in a chorus of amused but negative responses.[15]

Many people think the Bigfoot bull story is just that, a lot of bull. It is the consensus of many local residents that the Goonyak report was a hoax, as there was only one known alleged encounter which was highly sensational, to say the least. Adding to this suspicion is the fact that no one ever found the body of the slain Bigfoot—or the bull, for that matter.

If the incident never happened, how did the story make its way across much of northern Vermont? The answer may lie with Dr. James P. Chaplin, a professor at St. Michael's College in Vermont. He believes Goonyak tales have their genesis in present-day folklore and rumor; they are a form of modern myth in the making. The fact that there were several different versions of the tale supports Chaplin's assertion. For instance, in one story, Goonyak weighed 450 pounds, while another variant had Bigfoot putting on weight, ballooning up to 1,000 pounds. Such stories are very similar to accounts of lonely drivers picking up a mysterious hitchhiker who then vanishes in an unexplained way. A typical report appeared in the

Binghamton, NY Press, July 26, 1980:

> LITTLE ROCK (UPI)— Reports of a mysterious hitchhiker who talks about the second coming of Jesus Christ then disappears into thin air from moving cars has sparked the imagination of highway travelers and mystified the state police.
>
> Trooper Robert Roten said state police had had two reports—both on a Sunday—that a clean-cut, well-dressed hitchhiker had disappeared from cars traveling along highways near Little Rock.
>
> Efforts to find someone who actually saw the "highway apostle" proved fruitless. But Little Rock is apparently full of people who know someone who knows someone who had it happen to them.

It appears that the same social process—rumors, generated both the Goonyak tale and vanishing hitchhiker tales. These stories apparently fulfill psychological needs. Dr. Chaplin believes this is how Goonyak began. "It gives the person a sense of importance to pass along some news . . . especially news that is mysterious to explain." Chaplin thinks the Goonyak "myth" likely started with a deer hunter who may have "had a little too much Dutch courage (booze)."[16] Then the story distorts, being passed down and embellished upon, growing more wild and bizarre with retelling. Moreover, such tales cannot be traced to an original witness. None of the Goonyak stories ever identify the farmer invovled. Goonyak, like the hitchhiker, invariably is heard from a friend of a friend's mother's aunt's cousin. A common practice of professors teaching folklore and mythology is to tell one student a story and repeat it throughout the entire class. For example, the original story may be that two nuns walked into a local food market and were held up, struck over the head with a cantaloupe, and left for dead. As the story is retold from student to student, each is repeated in a slightly different way. By the time the last person hears it and is asked to repeat it, it wouldn't be at all unusual for him to tell of the nuns holding up the store and striking the cashier over the head with a cantaloupe.

It's important to emphasize here, that although some Bigfoot stories—and apparently all of the Goonyak accounts—spring from the same rumor seeds, most stories of this nature are usually easy to identify, as there is never any original witness. Such is not the case with the vast majority of Bigfoot reports investigated in New York and Vermont.

During July 1979, a man and his family were fishing the north bank of "East Bay" River in the town of West Haven. According to the witness, the group saw a hairy, man-like head peering over the bushes at them. His first thought was that it was a man, so he yelled at it. Whatever "it" was did not respond, and instead fled, running eastward. He could see its head bobbing behind the bushes, occasionally coming into view. It appeared to run in a very inhuman, bent-over manner. About a week later, the same family members returned to the fishing spot, only this time they took a gun. They reported a similar encounter, but the man decided against firing the weapon.[17]

The next several years saw a dry spell in Vermont, at least in terms of reports actually making their way into the hands of the media or researchers. It's probable that incidents did take place, but if no one reported it, for all intents and purposes, it never happened. To have a Bigfoot sighting, you need a Bigfoot or something that looks like a Bigfoot; next, a person in the vicinity at the same time who observes the creature and is willing to discuss it. Even then if the incident makes its way to a reporter or someone interested in Bigfoot who is willing to record the account, there's no guarantee that the reporter will write the story or the researcher will take it seriously enough to interview the witness.

In March 1983, Tinmouth, Vermont became the location of the next major creature encounter. In a letter to Professor Cook, a middle-aged couple related their intriguing experience:

> We were traveling slowly in a very rural area that was dotted with farms. I happened to be looking toward a low ridge to my left (East) when I saw what appeared to be a giant of a 'man' running (or walking quite swiftly) along this rocky ridge. The man was very nimble. I couldn't believe how quickly he was moving among the rocks

toward the high point on the ridge. . . . My wife and I were suddenly stunned when he stopped and turned facing us. His arms were much longer than a normal man's and he appeared to be much bigger—especially taller—than any man either of us had ever seen. It was very odd that this 'being' stopped for several minutes and remained motionless while he appeared to be looking down to the road toward us. Suddenly he raised his giant arms above his head and waved them several times. . . . We thought then that maybe someone was playing a prank. . . . (But) when he turned and continued along the ridge with the agility of a gymnast . . . I was convinced that this was no ordinary man. Soon he was gone from sight to the backside of the ridge. We waited . . . but he did not reappear.

Another incident was reported to Bigfoot investigator Ted Pratt by a man who wishes to be anonymous. It happened one spring night of 1984 in the Rutland County town of Chittenden. Pratt interviewed the man, a longtime hunter, who was genuinely frightened:

Last spring, a gentleman who is not willing to give his name, woke up during the night with some very loud screaming at his backdoor . . . he's really not afraid of anything, but he told me, . . . 'I just couldn't get out of bed. It was a horrible scream. It lasted . . . five to seven seconds.' And then he heard his cellar door being ripped off the hinges. His daughter . . . [lives] down the road . . . [and] also heard the scream . . . We looked over the area and we found one footprint, one handprint. . . . If this is so, this has to be the first act of aggression we've ever seen, at least in the state of Vermont.[18]

By the mid-1980s, interest in the creature's possible existence reached new levels of awareness. Two scientific conferences, organized by Professor Cook, were held on the campus of Vermont's Castleton State College. On April 24, 1985, an overflowing crowd gathered at the Florence Black Science Center to listen to witnesses and researchers recount data on Sasquatch. In attendance that evening was Ronald Lewis of Brandon, Vermont, a schoolteacher and founder of The New England Bigfoot/Sasquatch Research Alliance, which was organized to document regional creature sightings. George Greenough, the late publisher of the *Whitehall Independent*, summarized the conference in a May 1 article:

> ... The gathering last Wednesday evening, was the first of its kind in the area and Dr. Cook expressed his appreciation for the interest of the audience and urged them to push for legislative protection for such creatures as 'Sasquatch.' Information gathered by the serious study of the species could give valuable information regarding human development.

The success of the first conference led to a second held on November 25, yielding similar results. The topic captured the interest of many, as the sightings continued to roll in.

During April 1984 James Guyette began his usual routine as a newspaper deliverer around 5:30 a.m. by dropping off the morning papers for the Bellows Falls paperboys. While driving north that rainy morning on US Rt. 91 about 1½ miles below North Hartland and within sight of the Hartland Dam, a large, hairy "animal-man [had] come up the bank near the brook, walking fast down the road at an angle, maybe 100 yards away." Guyette said it went down the highway bank and up the other side, travelling westward, away from the Connecticut River.

"The animal-man looked tall and lanky with long arms swinging as he walked." It "had a head shaped like a helmet attached to a uniform in the back." Guyette stopped, trying to decipher what it was, and hoping the creature would return, but it "disappeared over the bank." Later, when trying to tell his wife what happened, the shaken Guyette broke down crying. During April 1985, a *Rutland Herald* newspaper article describing several Vermont Bigfoot sightings came to the attention of a neighbor who razzed him at the time of the sighting. Appearing at Guyette's door and showing him the article, he said, "I guess I owe you an apology." This prompted Guyette to phone Dr. Cook, who was mentioned in the article, and tell him about the Windsor County incident.[19]

Less than two months after Guyette's encounter, Hubbardton, Rutland County, was the scene of an unusual mxperience by Bruce Bateau and his mother, Mrs. Bernard F. Bateau.

From his bed Bruce heard noises similar to a cross between a shriek and a whistle about 3:30 a.m. Whatever was making the frightening sound seemed to be running away. The next day he and his mother walked along a favorite thick stand of pine trees. Glancing down, Bruce could see a series of large, naked human-like foot tracks, with an instep, but only three perceivable toes. The pines are just south of Monument Hill Road. Something else caught his attention; an extraordinary smell. The area near the prints gave off a musty/musky odor, like cologne but somewhat rotten. It gave him a strange feeling.[20]

Hubbardton was also the scene of a Bigfoot report sometime during the same year. A hairy Bigfoot-like creature was sighted by "J," a man who took such ridicule from his friends that he now insists on remaining anonymous. Dr. Cook learned of the incident through a friend of his who worked with "J" at a popular Rutland specialty store. Cook wrote the man, trying to get further details, but received no reply.[21]

Hubbardton remained a hotbed of Bigfoot activity during the same year. A man returning home from work said he spotted a huge, hairy ape-like creature in the northwestern corner of town. The man told a longtime friend and employee of the Castleton Post Office, Audrey Beam, that he saw a strange creature walking upright, near the edge of a cleared field. Professor Cook wrote the man two letters, but he chose not to respond.[22]

During that same year, near Hubbardton, in Clarendon, south of Rutland, a couple attending a party claimed to have seen a large, hairy ape-like creature early one morning near the junction of Rt. 7 and Rt. 103. Dr. Cook's neighbor, Edna Brown, heard the story from her visiting nurse. Cook decided to examine the story, as the couple claimed to be so disturbed that they reported it to the State Police, who seemed disbelieving. Cook immediately went to the State Police office off Rt. 7 north of Rutland.

> The officer that I talked to said, 'Yes, there was such a report, but if I had seen the type of people they were, I wouldn't have taken them seriously.' I said, do you mean they were 'hippie types?' He said, 'Yes.' Nor did he seem

to take me seriously.[23]

Concluding the 1984 cases were three encounters reported to well-known Vermont logging industry magnate, Hugo Meyer of Cabot, one of the largest property owners in the state. Through his network of contacts in the industry, Meyer heard of three sightings of a Bigfoot-type creature: two in Essex County, the other in Caledonia County.[24]

The first 1985 report occurred once again in Rutland County. On the snowy evening of March 4, in Clarendon Flats, Mrs. Dorothy Mason and son, Jeff, were inside their house when, as Mrs. Mason recounted:

> . . . I was looking out the window to see how much snow had fallen. I happened to notice some very large and unusual tracks about thirty feet from the window. . . . I called my son and we decided at that moment that we had better take some measurements . . . before the snow had filled them in. . . . They were sixteen inches in length, five inches in width and the span between each track was six feet.[25]

The shape of the prints impressed Dorothy; they were like a human foot, with a "definite big toe and three smaller ones that we could see very clearly and possibly one other." Dorothy didn't spot whatever made the tracks but surmised that "this creature . . . went right behind my car, across the lawn, and headed . . . westerly . . . [in the direction of] the river . . . over the mountain and towards West Rutland."[26]

During June 1985, two men relaxed in their boat while fishing on Foster Pond in the town of Peacham, Caledonia County. The pair, from the St. Johnsbury area, observed a hairy form, possibly two, on shore. At first glance they thought it to be a bear standing upright, and maneuvered the boat closer to get a better look. At that point the "bear" startled the men by turning and running off into a cedar tree swamp. At first it strode like a human, then surprised them by breaking into a run. The bottom of the feet were lighter colored than the rest of the animal.[27]

Perhaps the most interesting 1985 case occurred on the evening of September 20. Frank "Fron" Grabowski III and Bob

Davis were at the home of Ed and Theresa Davis, some two miles west of West Rutland. Frank, a West Rutland eighth-grader, was sitting on the front porch with Bob, when several family members and friends heard strange grunts and a shriek. Walking up a dirt road to investigate, the pair spotted a "gorilla-like" creature, standing upright, advancing toward them. Although concerned by its actions, Bob didn't get the feeling the creature would hurt them so long as they didn't confront it.[28] Bob said, at about 8:30, "I started walking up the road and saw a black image. It was taller than me and ran like a human." Initially, the pair said it threw stones at them, but when it came close to the house, they turned the tables and started throwing stones back. It then fled. Bob said the seven-foot-tall creature had black skin under its eyes, but couldn't describe more detail. Meanwhile, brother Al was circling behind the house to see what might be "pranking" them, situating himself along a back ledge overlooking the gravel road to get ahead of whatever, or more likely, whoever it was. Al poised himself, ready to grab the culprit. That's when he spotted it and froze in his tracks.

> . . . It was big . . . humungous in the shoulders . . . God, to me, it had like a monkey run to it . . . like long stride foot . . . the way it was twisting the shoulders.[29]

Ed Davis, nearby when all the commotion was taking place, didn't actually see anything. Like Al, he heard bizarre noises and experienced a "gassy or swampy smell" of "something really nauseating."[30] Al said it as a "wicked" odor smelling "unreal." Another friend, Roscoe Jones, saw it.

Frank discovered at least six large tracks indented into the hard gravel road where the creature was spotted. Despite the Friday night incident, and finding the unusual tracks Saturday, no one contacted the media or police. It fact, the events of that weekend might never have been made public, if not for two teachers at the West Rutland High School. On Monday, Frank told some classmates, and soon it was all around school. Teachers Linda Barker and Mel Loomis, students of Dr. Cook years earlier, knew Frank as a truthful, sixteen-year-old, and contacted Cook. By late Monday afternoon, Cook was at the site, making plaster casts of the prints and taking photos. Cook said the prints were clearly defined, estimating the creature's weight at 400 pounds. The fourteen-inch tracks measured seven inches in width.[31]

Frank also said that something broke into the chicken coops at the nearby Burton "Burt" McCullough farm on the Proctor Road killing several chickens about the same time. Tracks similar to those found near the Davis home were discovered there as well.[32]

It is interesting to note that, although the media often takes blame for sensationalizing Bigfoot accounts, an opposite process was working in this case. Dr. Cook thought if the local media reported the story, it might encourage other witnesses to come forward. The *Rutland Herald* published an article on the incident, Wednesday, September 25, on page twenty. The "'Bigfoot' Seen in West Rutland" story took its place that day among such headlines on the same page as "Squirted Soap Spurs Suit," "Adult Activities in Castleton," and "Otter Valley Holds Raft Race." Cook added that they were not going to published it at first, fearing it might hurt their reputation. Only when Cook threatened to give the account to the *Burlington Free Press*, did the *Herald* publish it.[33] This is not intended to single out the *Herald*. In fact, the paper has done some excellent stories on Bigfoot sightings in the area. The point is—just because it's not in the papers doesn't mean there aren't such experiences.

Two months after the encounter near the Davis' West Rutland home, two boys were playing one evening about 6:30. They stood in the same dooryard as the anonymous Chittenden man who, the previous spring heard a "horrible scream" and found his cellar door (two-inch oak) ripped clean off. Investigator Ted Pratt picks up the story:

> These two young boys were out behind their house, playing . . . one of the boys turned around to look at something, and what they believe was another Sasquatch . . . thirty to forty feet from them. He was playing with his new BB-gun, so the natural reaction to seeing [it was to] . . . empty the gun.[34]

The boy then turned, making a dash for the house in what was likely near-record time. But that wasn't the end of it. The next morning, Thursday, November 21, Ricky Siefert and Corey St. Lawrence were sitting at the back of the daily school bus which picks them up about 8 a.m. As the bus was turning around in the parking lot of a nearby establishment, the two grade-schoolers saw something that looked out of place. Peering out the back window, Rickie could see a big, black hairy creature crossing the corner of the field north of the parking lot. Corey saw it too. Both were certain it wasn't a bear.[35] Corey's brother (about age eleven) tells of seeing a similar-looking animal within the past year and a half, near the St. Lawrence family home.[36]

The most recent Vermont activity was reported in October 1986, both sightings in Rutland County. On the first of the month, three students at Castleton State College, John Brandt, Kerry Bilda and George Dietrich were travelling to the West Rutland Grand Union along Rt 4A when they all spotted a 6½ to 7-foot creature at about 8 p.m. Brandt screamed, "Watch out, Holy Shit!" thrusting his body backwards fearing a collision. Bilda swerved into the left lane and accelerated as the figure continued walking west to east on the right side of the pavement. Bilda and Brandt decided to turn around, over Dietrich's objections, but nothing else was seen or smelled. The incident happened near the "West Rutland" sign on the south side of the road about two miles west of town.[37]

Had their window been down as they passed the creature, Brandt said he could have reached out and touched it. Its body had collie-length hair while the face was virtually hairless with deep-set eyes and high cheekbones. The skin appeared white in color.

The trio were most puzzled over its nonchalant behavior. The creature did not move out of harm's way or flinch as the car passed by. Dr. Cook only learned of the sighting through his students who knew the men. It may be significant that this encounter occurred almost simultaneously with the sighting by Susan Cook, near the same spot, but coming from the opposite direction. The site was within 300 feet or less from the encounter of September 20, 1985.[38]

On Sunday, October 27, 1986 at about 9 p.m., two Castleton State College freshman girls sighted a Bigfoot-like creature while southbound on Rt. 30 in the town of Poultney, midway between Castleton Corners and the town. Jill Cortwright and passenger Cathy Quill both let out loud screams at the same moment. They both observed a huge creature crouched on the right side of the road, its backside facing them. Jill said its hair was "like a bear," but both were emphatic that it wasn't a bear. After Jill speeded up, the pair was too frightened to turn around. Being freshmen, neither girl was aware of Dr. Cook's Bigfoot research. Quill also said the creature's hair was "messy, not smooth like a bear." There were also thin hair patches on the buttocks. Like the previous sighting, it paid no attention to them.[39]

On February 11, 1987, two Castleton State College students reported finding large tracks in the snow. The pair was cross-country skiing in the East Poultney area, when they came across the barefoot trail.[40]

Some may consider it far-fetched that Bigfoot creatures could exist in the United States since no hard evidence, such as a body or bones, has ever been found. However, the Vermont catamount or "panther" as it is commonly called, has been officially 'extinct' here for over a century. Yet, there are continual sightings and in some cases, even animal killings attributed to such creatures. Still, Vermont Fish and Wildlife officials insist that the catamount does not roam the Green Mountain State. If the catamount has avoided capture or being shot for over a hundred years, is it that incredible that Bigfoot creatures could elude detection? The most recent possible panther case occurred in late October of 1991. The November 12th *Rutland Herald* published a front-page story on the incident:

> ORWELL—Speculation has increased that catamounts again roam Vermont's hills, following a series of mysterious attacks that led to the death of 15 head of cattle.
>
> Farmer Kenneth Pope and veterinarian Kent Anderson both believe an attack by a large cat is the most likely explanation for a pattern of mutilation that severely

injured 14 heifers and one cow on a Sunday, Tuesday and Wednesday in late October. However, neither Pope nor Anderson has ruled out some other cause.

Meanwhile, within the past two years residents in Orwell and Bridport have reported seeing panthers, as the mountain lions are commonly known in Vermont. Fish and Wildlife Department officials insist that the last panther in Vermont died more than a century ago, but all the witnesses insist that the massive animal involved was definitely not a bobcat.

The incidents took place at a farm in a relatively wild section of Orwell, which is in the Champlain Valley in the southwestern corner of Addison County.

The attacks occurred in a barn that is remote from the farmhouse. After the third incident, Pope removed his cattle to a neighbor's barn, and he said he probably will not use his barn again until Spring.

One heifer was attacked on Sunday, but Pope thought the deep puncture wounds and scratches came from the animal getting loose and running into a barbed wire fence, Anderson said. On Tuesday, four more cattle had their faces attacked, according to Pope.

That night, Pope closed and locked the doors to the barn. But something got in through a window and damaged the remaining cattle, he said.

Anderson was called in on Thursday to examine the results of the attacks, which left the cattle maimed but not dead. He found injuries so severe that the cattle had to be put down, resulting in what Pope said was a $10,000 loss.

"We found some deep scratches and lacerations," Anderson said, in some cases so severe that most of the flesh had been torn from the faces. Facial bones had been crushed into facial sinuses, by something so strong it must have weighed at least 100 pounds, he said.

"There were deep scratches on the face and on the nose," Anderson said. "I wouldn't rule out dogs, but it wasn't as likely," he said, given the number of scratch wounds and the absence of biting wounds anywhere else than on the front of the head.

There has been local speculation about some sort of satanic ritual being involved, Anderson said, but an attack by humans seemed unlikely to him. It would have taken three people, he said: one with a hammer, one with a knife, and one with something like a sharpened gardening hand rake.

"My best guess would be something along the lines of a bear or a large cat," Anderson said. But no rabies has been reported in the state that would make a normally placid bear attack something in a barn, he said.

The cat family's habit of playing with it prey might help to explain the pattern of attacking without killing, and a catamount might have been attracted by the smell of the de-horning wounds, (sic) he said. "I can't say that's what did it," he said. "That just seems to be more likely."

Game Warden Eugene Gaiotti, who was called about the incidents, said, "We really don't know what killed those cows. I thought possibly dogs, but then after I heard several stories, I really don't know what did it."

Orwell sheep farmer Jean Beck said she did not know of any attacks at her farm or elsewhere in Orwell. "There's been a lot of talk about it," she said. "A lot of people think it's a catamount."

One reason for the theory is that Orwell resident Sharon Pinsonneault reported seeing a catamount on August 21 crossing Route 22A in an aera of steep, rocky ledges in Benson near the Benson-Orwell line.

"When I first saw it, I had no idea what it was," Pinsonneault said. She could not see its head, other than to know that the face was more rounded than pointed.

"The thing I remember was the long tail," Pinsonneault said. "It almost reached the ground and then it curled up in an arch."

It was only after talking to a friend who had read an article about catamounts that Pinsonneault recalled a trip to Montpelier in the summer, during which she had seen the stuffed 19th century Wardsboro panther. "When I thought back on it, I thought 'Yeah—same color, same size," she said.

Ronald Lewis of Brandon, the president of the Northeast Panther Research Alliance, said Pinsonneault's sighting was only one of a series of such reports that have come in steadily in recent years. Since many people do not speak of what they have seen, he plans to contact all the state's deer reporting stations this fall to let hunters know they can call 247-5913 about sightings.

In Bridport, which Lewis said could be well within the

same territory as Orwell for a catamount, a hired hand on the Charles Deering farm said she had seen a catamount regularly over a five-week period two years ago.

Mary Charland said that one morning she came down through her dooryard and watched the cat pass the road "within inches" while she reamined frozen in terror.

Once she saw the cat rolling in the dirt road, taking a dirt bath to drive off fleas. "He's a beautiful cat. He's big and has a long tail and long legs and a beautiful head," she said.

Deering said that in August, someone riding by the farm on an all-terrain vehicle said he and a friend had watched a catamount for about an hour.

Deering said he had seen the cat once about two years ago. It was about four feet long, had a five-foot stride, and was "like a mountain lion" in color and appearance, he said.

In Cornwall, Mary Stevenson said that in January 1990 she watched through her back window while something she thought was a deer rolled on it back in the snow. When it got up, she saw "it had a great long tail that came down almost to the ground and bent."

"I have seen a bobcat out back several years ago, but this was ever so much bigger than that," Stevenson said.

The State Fish and Wildlife Department has discounted catamount sightings, arguing that there would be more carcasses of catamounts and deer killed by catamounts if they had returned to the state. But spokesman John Hall said the many seemingly credible reports have led officials to wonder if people who tried to raise young mountain lions as pets had released them in Vermont once they became unmanageable adults.

Joan Cunningham of Benson, a breeder of wolf hybrid dogs who is now studying for a doctorate in wild animal behavior, said she does not think the pet-catamount-gone-wild theory is credible. There are almost no big cats being kept by private individuals, she said, except for one tiger she knows of in Montana.

References:

*We are indebted to Dr. Warren L. Cook, Professor of History & Anthropology at Castleton State College, Castleton, VT, who compiled and unselfishly made available most of the reports in this chapter. The quote by Hilary Evans at the beginning of the chapter appears in "Falling into Place," *Fortean Times*, Issue No. 41, Winter, 1983, p. 22. In the article Evans warns of the dangers of pattern-making, but pleads for more adventurous hypotheses.

1. Interview between Dr. Warren Cook and John Rowell.
2. Story told to John Rowell by Bill Lyford. Rowell, in turn, repeated it to Dr. Cook. Mr. Lyford is now deceased, thus a follow-up interview is not possible.
3. Transcript of a taped interview between Dr. Cook and John Rose of Castleton Corners, VT, August, 1983.
4. Green, John, *Sasquatch: The Apes Among Us*. Seattle, WA: Hancock House, 1978, p. 231.
5. Personal interview by Dr. Cook with anonymous Rutland area businessman.
6. Transcript of a tape made by Dr. Cook on August 16, 1978, for Paul Bartholomew.
7. Interview between Dr. Cook and the anonymous couple involved.
8. Warren Cook learned of this incident through neighbor David Mason. Cook then talked with James Ingalls via telephone.
9. Information supplied by Bill Brann.
10. Ibid.
11. Transcription by Paul Bartholomew of the second "Sasquatch, alias Bigfoot Conference" held at Castleton State College, Castleton, VT, November 25, 1985
12. Ibid.
13. Ibid.
14. Duffy, Kevin, "'Goonyak' Reports Debunked, But Rumors of Its Exploits Captivate Northern Vermont." *Rutland Herald*, November 30, 1978.
15. Ibid.
16. Ibid.
17. Interview between Dr. Cook and the anonymous Fair Haven man.
18. Paul Bartholomew transcript of the November 25, 1985 second "Sasquatch, alias Bigfoot Conference" at Castleton State College.
19. Phone interview between Dr. Cook and James Guyette, and several months later in person by Collamer Abbott.
20. Interview by Dr. Cook with Bruce Bateau.
21. Conversation between Warren Cook and a family employee working in the same company as "J."
22. Dr. Cook's personal file on the case.
23. Quoting Dr. Cook's personal case file.

24. Interview between Dr. Cook and Hugo Meyer.
25. Paul Bartholomew transcript of the November 25, 1985 second "Sasquatch, alias Bigfoot Conference" at Castleton State College.
26. Ibid.
27. Interview between John Rowell and Warren Cook. Rowell was told the story by a man from Wells River (a part of Newberry, VT) who heard it from a man who heard it from a witness.
28. Personal interview by Dr. Cook and several of the witnesses at the scene, September 23, 1985. Also, transcript of interview at the location between Paul Bartholomew and Frank "Fron" Grabowski Jr., Ed and Al Davis. Also, Paul Bartholomew's final report on the case.
29. Transcript of interview by Paul Bartholomew and Frank "Fron" Grabowski Jr., Ed and Al Davis, September 23, 1985.
30. Ibid.
31. "'Big Foot' Seen in West Rutland," *Rutland Herald,* September 25, 1985, p. 20.
32. Personal interviews at the Davis home by Warren Cook and Paul Bartholomew, September 23, 1985, with Ed and Al Davis, and Frank "Fron" Grabowski.
33. Personal interviews by Paul and Bob Bartholomew with Dr. Cook.
34. Paul Bartholomew transcript of the November 25, 1985 second "Sasquatch, alias Bigfoot Conference" as Castleton State College.
35. Interview between Dr. Cook and the witness.
36. Ibid.
37. Dr. Cook's personal file. Cook was informed of the sighting by Joe Antell (his current student) who was told of it by his Adams Hall suitemate, Steven O'Conner, a personal friend of the witness.
38. Dr. Cook's interview with his daughter, Susan Cook.
39. Dr. Cook's personal interview with both witnesses.
40. From Dr. Cook's personal files.

Chapter 8

WHAT IS IT?

Now that we've tracked the history of Bigfoot from ancient Indian legends and folktales through modern sightings, let's see what we can come up with in the way of theories. The ides are many and varied, and the following is a list of possible candidates:

1. A large, hairy humanoid, or prehistoric "human," of a species unknown to science.
2. A psychic projection akin to poltergeists and hauntings.
3. Misidentifications of known animals, such as bears.
4. Escaped gorillas or chimpanzees from zoos or circuses.
5. Pranksters dressed in costumes, etc.
6. An unknown creature with a highly evolved set of defense mechanisms, allowing it to adapt to its surroundings in the same way that a chameleon changes color to blend into its immediate environment.
7. Interdimensional entities that come from another plane or world (whatever that means), occasionally entering our sphere of life.
8. Bigfoot as extraterrestrials.
9. Demonic manifestations.
10. Mass media sensationalism.
11. Need-fulfillment. It's fun and exciting to see Bigfoot—especially in a world where mystical beliefs are becoming replaced by science.
12. Hallucinations.
13. Mentally unbalanced people.

14. Mass hysteria.
15. Bigfoot as myth.
16. A phenomenon that is incomprehensible at present. Our science is nowhere near evolved enough to try and figure it out. It would be comparable to a caveman trying to explain a jet plane.

Now let's examine these possibilities one by one. We will start with what we consider the least likely, then work our way down.

Obviously, pranksters haven't been dressing in animal skins or rented ape costumes since the days of the Indians just to scare people. This theory couldn't possibly account for Bigfoot's suppose height, strength and depth of footprints. Even the "wild man" of the Adirondacks didn't have people convinced for long that he was anything but an ordinary man covered with animal skins.

The rationalization that all such creatures are zoo escapees boggles the mind. If this were the case, every zoo in the country (or indeed the world) would be empty of gorillas and chimps. It's a very pat "logical explanation," but doesn't hold up under close scrutiny.

There can be no doubt that bears have occasionally been mistaken for Bigfoot. Nonetheless, they do not walk on their hind legs, although they may rear up when alarmed or looking for food. They never run on *two* legs; they're quite incapable of standing erect for any period of time. Since Bigfoot it always reported as being bipedal, we can rule out bears or other animals in nearly every case.

Bigfoot as demons seems to fit under the category that you can always find enough evidence to support any hypothesis. Despite how unlikely it may seem, its possibility should be acknowledged. Proponents of Bigfoot as demons include some fundamentalist Christians who believe we are in the last days of the earth—that the end-time is near—and all types of evil manifestations will appear. How much more scary can you get than a big hairy monster running around frightening people half to death. On the other side of the coin, if Bigfoot is an end-time demon, encounters date back far back into Indian lore, and the end-time is sure taking an awful long time getting here. Another strike against this theory is that Bigfoot is rarely reported to harm people, and in some cases appears to be downright friendly.

If most witnesses are crazy or unbalanced, then mental illness is much more prevalent than is commonly believed. Most appear sane, "normal" people from all age groups and diverse occupations. A large portion of the reports involve multiple witnesses. Two cases from New York involved close range multiple sightings by law enforcement officials. Neither case could have been a misidentification and both cases were investigated first-hand. For instance, consider the incident where two Washington County law enforcement personnel saw a 7½-foot tall, hairy creature run across the road in front of their car at about 4:30 a.m. in rural Whitehall. Besides being within close proximity, after crossing the road it easily scaled a steep cliff and disappeared into a heavily wooded, mountainous region. No human could have performed such a feat. The second report involved two different police officers in Whitehall at about midnight on August 25, 1976, when a Bigfoot stood for about a minute within twenty-five feet of one of the men. The other officer saw the creature from a distance. Large naked footprints were also found in farmer Harry Diekel's cornfield nearby. In both cases, either two sets of trained and respected law officers with everything to lose and nothing to gain were hoaxing at the risks of their reputations and jobs, or they observed what they said they saw. Misinterpretation appears virtually impossible in both cases, and mass hallucination seems highly unlikely.

For a classic example of misidentifications that deal with the lighter side of Bigfoot searching, it is interesting to observe how, occasionally, a person's imagination can get the best of them. The following is taken from Adirondack history expert Fred Styles's book *Old Days-Old Ways*:

> My neighbor Hail Hall came to see me one day. About everybody around this time was seeing Bigfoot and believing implicitly that such a thing existed.
> Now Hail is a man who will tell you a story of his diggins and of course they don't always turn out as they expected, but he has found enough of the real good stuff,

so he needn't be ashamed of a surprise once in a while.

This day he had been digging not far from the water and looking up all of a sudden, he saw a giant form about 10 feet tall with a great bushy head. He threw the metal detector down and went galloping off at great speed til he had gone some distance. Then stopping, he realized he had thrown his detector down when he had started running. Now that detector had cost quite a large sum of money and so he tip-toed slowly back to retrieve it, but ready to run off again, if Bigfoot was still there. So carefully he retraced his steps till he could see his detector. Glancing towards the place where Bigfoot had been, there he was and he was wiggling his head back and forth —it was a very large porcupine, munching on a limb about 10 feet up a tree. And I guess he believes as I do, if the people who see Bigfoot had time to look more closely, they would find something which could be explained.

But for a real queer animal, it would be hard to beat this report.

There is little doubt that media sensationalism does play a role in Bigfoot reports; the question is to what extent? We live in an information age where TV, newspapers, radio and computers offer us nearly instant contact with the most remote parts of the world. If someone reports seeing Bigfoot, large portions of a population are in a position of hearing about it within minutes or hours—at the least—days.

The media hypothesis raises the question of which came first, the sighting or the media account. Surely, before any wave of Bigfoot reports, there has to be an initial sighting to get reported in the media. Although hysteria may be able to partially explain the tendency of accounts to occur in "waves," and no doubt anything that half resembles Bigfoot can be easily misinterpreted by anyone in the right frame of mind, it's naive to think all are.

The idea that Bigfoot reports are generated by need-fulfillment is an interesting one. All of the organs in our body serve a purpose, or, as in the case of the appendix, are believed to have once been purposeful. Functionalism contends that not only do we physically evolve in ways that best meet survival needs, but socially we evolve the same way. Hence, at funerals, friends gather to pay respects to the deceased. More importantly, this gathering of friends serves a purpose; to comfort each other, especially the family in a time of great psychological need.

Let's face it. To see Bigfoot or banter around exotic theories that it may be the missing link or even extraterrestrial provides escapism from the problems of everyday life. It's fun, exciting, adventurous to think that a Bigfoot-like creature could be roaming the woods.

Throughout history, man has believed in the supernatural. This is simple to explain. A lightning bolt, earthquake, rain, sunshine; most everything had a mysterious explanation. Once we became "civilized," organized science developed. In a world where religious beliefs are eroding and science is taking all the "fun" out of heretofore mysteries like sea serpents and comets, Bigfoot offers us the opportunity to act on "faith." Bigfoot research groups have been formed. Some meet regularly, usually discussing recent evidence as a way of strenthening their faith that the creature exists. It is not unlike churchgoers meeting weekly to reinfoce their faith in the mysterious —something they believe in—want to believe in, but can't actually prove.

At first glance the idea of Bigfoot as an extraterrestrial sounds far-fetched. A closer inspection shows there are several dozen Bigfoot-like creature reports in either direct association with UFOs, or where UFOs were seen in the same vicinity within a short time before or after the incident. Researcher Mark Moravec has even compiled an entire catalog of just such reports. The following is a typical example, if there is such a thing as a "typical" UFO-Bigfoot encounter. It was reported at about 3 p.m. in mid-September 1975 in Waterloo, Indiana.

> Farmer watched out a window and noticed a red light the size of a car headlight in a soybean field about 75 yards away. In an area illuminated by a houselight, he also saw a large, bipedal 'animal' which walked towards the object with a swaying motion.[1]

Coincidence? Perhaps. But there are enough of these reports that seem to go beyond chance. In another incident, a woman living near Cincinnati, Ohio woke up in the middle of the afternoon on October 21, 1973 and observed six bright stationary lights, alternating between blue and silver. She said that they were about two yards from her window, while in the backyard she noticed a "shield of light" shaped like a bell-jar. The light was about seven feet high and enveloped an "apelike creature" with a head and snout, no neck and a large waist area. Its arms were described as moving up and down in a rigid motion. The incident lasted about five minutes.[2]

The next incident was reported in early December 1974 at about 10:30 p.m. near Frederic, Wisconsin.

> Dairy farmer driving home saw a 'strange being' inside an enclosure the shape of a bell jar and six feet across. The being was six feet tall, covered in reddish-brown fur, had hair sticking out the sides of its head, a moderate length neck and calf-like ears sticking straight out at least 3". The being had its arms up in the air and his eyes showed very intense fright. When the object seemed to approach the witness' car, the inside of the car became very dark. The object then took off with a swish.[3]

Is Bigfoot an ET? Although such reports would indicate a definite possibility, many things don't make sense. In most UFO-Bigfoot association cases, the large, hairy creatures usually act like an animal and not an ET. Often they grunt, growl and run around in a manner unbecoming of an ET. This same argument can be taken as favoring the Bigfoot-ET hypothesis. Critics of extraterrestrials often contend that most UFOnauts appear too human-like—too close to our science fiction expectations of how ETs should look and act.

Also, if such creatures are alien, what are they doing roaming the woods and hovering above remote fields in the middle of the night? Some researchers feel this association may involve some unknown experiment, perhaps biological. The UFO-Bigfoot theory offers much food for thought, but little conclusive evidence.

The possibility of Bigfoot as an interdimensional animal is intriguing. It's a theory that looks good on paper, and can answer several sticky questions. Unfortunately, its virtually impossible to "prove."

Throughout the years, thousands of seemingly level-headed people swear they've seen something, yet no absolute physical proof remains. If these creatures come from another plane of existence, the interdimensional theory can go a long way toward bridging the gap.

In the Bigfoot literature there are a relatively small number of well-documented cases in which the creature is seen at a close distance by seemingly reliable observers, and it definitely acts unlike a flesh and blood animal. In autumn 1968, near Point Isabel, Ohio, two men and a boy claimed to have seen a 'monster' rise up and walk toward them from tall brush nearby. It was about 10 p.m. It stood some ten feet tall and four feet wide at the shoulders. Its hairy body was described as having ape-like arms, its eyes glowing, teeth prominent and protruding, ears pointed. After losing sight of the creature, it was later spotted nearby. When one of the men shot at it, it let out a loud scream and was immediately enveloped in a white mist. Within a minute there was no trace of the strange mist or the creature—nothing.[4]

If Bigfoot is from another dimension, this could explain the large volume of reports, yet the absence of bones, bodies or fossils which are never found. It can also explain why footprints have been seen in a number of cases that suddenly end in the middle of nowhere. It could also explain why, on several occasions, hunters or witnesses protecting themselves from a perceived threat, have shot at the creature yet were unable to kill it. Take the next case, reported at about 10 p.m, February 1974 in Uniontown, Pennsylvania. Mark Moravec summarizes the event:

> A woman thought she heard dogs upsetting the garbage, so she went outside with a shotgun. A few feet away was a seven-foot-tall, hair-covered, ape-like creature which immediately raised both hands above its head. The witness fired the shotgun at the creature's gut but it just 'diappeared in a flash of light . . . just like someone taking a picture.' Her son-in-law heard the shot and proceeding to her residence, saw a group of four or five seven-foot-tall, hair-covered, ape-like creatures with long arms and 'fire red eyes that glowed.' He fired two shots and ran into the house.[5]

Before fully embracing the interdimensional theory, several questions need answering. Why are they visiting this dimension in the first place and what is it they're doing in the woods? Also, if they have this interdimensional ability, why is it that in the majority of cases they are seen leaving areas in a conventional manner, such as running. Why not just pop into the other existence if they feel threatened? Also, just what is another dimension and does it exist?

Research on mass hysteria indicates that whenever a group of people with common beliefs is stressed while simultaneously in an ambiguous environment such as a dark wooded area, and something vague is seen or heard (a mysterious noise, bushes rustling), extreme tension builds to the point where they need to resolve the strain. They want to know one way or the other. If, for instance, it is just a friend walking nearby, they can relax. Or if it is Bigfoot, they can flee. Yet, no one likes to make a fool of themselves by running away screaming when it turns out to be their six-year-old brother walking through the nearby brush. However, no doubt many people camping out in wooded areas are in a Bigfoot "mind set." Under these conditions they would become highly suggestible and more prone to misinterpretations. If people are camping in an area where Bigfoot reportedly lives and a raccoon climbs a nearby tree making a noise, one of the group may see the two eyes in the darkness standing seven feet off the ground, staring at him. Such eyes can appear large, shiny and pink or red at night when someone points a flashlight at them. Within a second his imagination fills in the outline of a Bigfoot body in the branches. As the witness panics and flees screaming, nervous companions who may be in a similar Bigfoot frame of mind take flight also.

A classic case of mass hysteria occurred in Matoon, Illinois in 1944.[6] Between August 31 and September 12, police logged twenty-five separate reports of citizens claiming to have been sprayed with a mysterious incapacitating "gas" by some-one dubbed the "phantom anesthetist." The first report was highly ambiguous, but received sensational hometown coverage. A woman stated that someone had opened her bedroom window at night while she simultaneously experienced minor leg paralysis and smelled an unusual odor. It was concluded that because over 90% of the people affected were females who were below the general population in wealth and education level, the victims were less critical in evaluating the situation. Based on the initial ambiguous report and the heightened anxiety levels it created, normally occurring events (seeing a possible prowler or a shadowy figure at night), less critical Matoon females redefined normally occurring physical reactions (heart palpitations caused by nervousness or minor temporary limb paralysis), and chemical odors from nearby factories. Despite extensive tests no trace of the "gas" was found and no one ever got a close or clear glimpse of the gasser. Because of the initial sensational rumor of a gasser on the loose, normal events were redefined. Thus before, sleeping women may not have normally paid much attention to chemical odors from the factories. But scared that the gasser might have been in the neighborhood, normally present odors were perceived as unusual. Believing this may have been caused by the gasser, kids playing or an unusual window reflection in the darkness could have easily been mistaken for the gasser, given the nervous frame of mind the Matoon women were in.

It seems probable that some Bigfoot sightings are the result of mass hysteria, but certainly not all. The question is to what extent? Too many cases involve multiple witnesses who saw the creature clearly at very close range (within 30 yards); some within a few feet. Several of the cases we have investigated involved observations by trained observers—police officers. On the other hand, it is an indisputable fact of psychology that eye-witness testimony, even at close range, is highly inaccurate. Year after year, study after study has confirmed and reconfirmed this. This is a major reason why most psychologists and sociologists reject Bigfoot sightings or are at the least, extreme skeptics. This is an understandable view for one to take given that no one to date has produced a body, fossil or bones. All we have is eye-witness testimony and footprints—and prints can be faked. A fossil, body or bones can't be faked in this day and age without scientists determining it as a hoax. Yet, what about the case against mass hysteria? Large naked footprints are found in the vicinity of sightings and sometimes track for miles, often appearing to have been made by someone or something much heavier than a human. Are there that many pranksters around who will go to such extreme lengths just for a joke. Why are so few jokers uncovered? Further, most sightings do not necessarily involve people who are poor and uneducated, as was the case in Matoon, Illinois. And the behavior of the creature does not fulfill witness expectations of what a Bigfoot should do. Instead of screaming or threatening the witnesses, more often than not it acts too nonchalant, almost apathetic. Definitely not how Bigfoot is portrayed in the movies.

Could Bigfoot be a myth? The scientific community has yet to accept the existence of the creature as anything but a myth. Bob Bartholomew helped to provide some insight as to why few scientists are willing to believe that Bigfoot could be a 'real' being:

> Seemingly honest, intelligent, mentally healthy people worldwide report encounters with supernatural creatures daily. Malaysians meet Toyl spirits who are typically just a few inches tall. The Ojibway Indians of Ontario, Canada continue to see Thunderbirds the size of airplanes, while modern-day encounters with Bunyips have been reported by Australian aborigines. The numerous animist cultures who believe in various indwelling nature spirits, frequently report encountering such entities. In many Western countries, Bigfoot-like creatures are sighted annually. What does it all mean? Is there some deep-seated psychological need to believe in 'monsters'— so much so that our imaginations create them? Could these beings actually exist as some unknown life form evolving remarkable abilities which allow it to elude capture? Could these sightings be of creatures from another dimension or planet? There is fascinating circumstantial evidence that these creatures exist.
>
> At the lest, this study provides insights into the making of a modern myth and helps to dispel the erroneous belief that many witnesses or believers in 'monsters' are mentally unbalanced. At best, if true, it documents one of the most startling and important events in human history. While I *hope* that Bigfoot and other phantom creatures exist, and find much of the evidence intriguing,

I cannot accept their reality until concrete proof is uncovered that will convince the scientific community; nothing short of a body, bones, or fossilized remains. Eye-witness testimony, footprints, ambiguous hair strands, and photographs are interesting, but unconvincing, unacceptable scientific evidence. People once reported fairy and witch sightings by the thousands. There were even 'abductions' to Fairyland and witch Sabbaths. Similar parallels can be made with the widespread belief in spiritualism during the latter nineteenth century. While the notion that fairies or witches exist today seems laughable, the point is—seemingly honest, reliable people raised in an environment that promotes the reality of fairies and witches, saw what they expected and wanted to see. Even hallucinations reflected the prevailing belief. This does not mean that Bigfoot does not exist. But it does help to explain why the scientific community has yet to accept Bigfoot's existence. Remarkable claims require clear, noncircumstantial evidence. Time, and adherence to the scientific method will ultimately determine whether Bigfoot exists or if it belongs to the realm of folklore and social psychology, as a monster of the human mind.

The defense mechanism hypothesis seems logical. Just as certain fish, frogs and lizards naturally change color to blend in with their immediate surroundings as a means of protection from attack, Bigfoot creatures may have evolved with similar but not completely understood mechanisms. This line of thought could explain why so many people claim they've seen the creature, yet searches of the vicinity soon after usually produce no further encounters and never a body or bones.

You may be thinking to yourself, well, if this creature can change color and possibly do other things we don't fully understand to elude capture, why would so many people see it in the first place? Well, as in the case of fish and lizards, the species that have this mechanism cannot instantly blend into their surroundings. It takes time to adjust.

The possibility of mechanisms we don't understand makes for interesting speculation. This could explain footprints, fecal matter, strange hair fibers apparently unattributable to any known species. Yet no one has ever brought in a Bigfoot. This theory doesn't answer what happens to such creatures when they die—and we assume they must die—as every organism known to man eventually does. Some researchers theorize that when Bigfeet die, they bury their dead, toss them off tall cliffs in remote areas, even eat the corpses. These explanations seem far-fetched, although all possibilities must be considered.

The psychic projection theory has been made prominent by writers Jerome Clark and Loren Coleman. It postulates that our thoughts can somehow take on a physical form, at least temporarily. Dr. Gary Levine, teacher of social sciences at Columbia-Greene Community College in Hudson, New York, has personally investigated many UFO and Bigfoot cases, and subscribes to this theory. "It seems to be a paranormal phenomenon which is related to psychic powers . . . Some people who are psychic can draw the creature to them."

Levine has no patience with the "apeman" theory. What you're dealing with, he says, "is something that has no basis in evolution. It's not an animal that's been somehow hiding in the mountains for thousands of years and then suddenly comes down. But it is here, and it's drawn to us in a psychic fashion. It appears to be a creation, a projection, of our collective imaginations. It has a form, but our perception of it is exactly what we think it should look like."

Clark and Coleman put it this way:

> If the otherworld is really the domain of the collective unconscious imprinted on the 'psi field,' creating in each cultural frame of reference a dream world . . . fixed in the psychic realm, then. . . . Where peasants were kidnapped into fairyland and mystics were transported into heaven, today UFO contactees are whisked off to Venus, a world as full of scientific marvels as the others were of supernatural ones.[7]

This theory can explain why footprints often end in the middle of fields, the lack of physical proof, and the variety of Bigfoot descriptions all over the world. The stuff of science fiction? Perhaps. But consider the following account from Roachdale, Indiana, August 29 1972:

> One night in August at (10 p.m.) a woman and her infant son heard a deep growl. One and a half hours earlier

> a luminous object had alighted over the neighbor's cornfield, hovered briefly, and then 'just sort of blew up' leaving no traces. During the next few nights the couple heard strange pounding noises and glimpsed an enormously broad-shouldered, six-foot-tall, black and hairy, bipedal creature fleeing into the cornfields. It smelled rotten like 'dead animals or garbage.' It stood like a man but would run on all fours, never leaving tracks. Sometimes, 'it looked like you could see through it.'[8]

In addition to the few but well-documented and persistent reports of "see through" Bigfeet, some people have definitely reported having more than their fair share of Bigfoot and UFO activity. In early October 1973, near Galveston, Indiana, a fisherman watched an ape-like figure apparently observing him from a distance. Minutes later, after he lost the creature from sight, it touched his shoulder.

> The witness whirled his head around and the creature ran away with amazing swiftness, leaping over a ditch and disappearing into the woods. Shortly afterwards a glowing bronze object shot into the sky, fading away quickly. The following evening the witness and four friends drove to the spot, trailed all the way by a white, glowing starlike light which disappeared near a bridge not far from the original creature sighting area . . . the eight to nine-foot-tall creature was in tall weeds, standing motionless as if in a trance (despite the witnesses yelling and throwing rocks at it) and giving off a 'musty' odor. Oddly its presence did not seem to disturb the crickets, frogs and other wildlife, and the observer's flashlight beams seemed somehow 'weaker' on the creature . . . (which) disappeared while the witnesses moved their vehicles from the road. One of the witnesses had an eight-year history of a dozen UFO and psychic experiences—including a flashlight communication with an orange glow in the sky, and a vivid 'dream' of standing aboard a UFO and conversing mentally with a humanoid figure with a large bald head.[9]

Although it's an interesting possibility, psychic projection is still unproven. It may have a great deal of circumstantial evidence going for it, but it has not been shown to exist. In fact, whether or not something as basic as ESP exists is at present the subject of intense scientific debate, accepted by some, but a majority of the scientific community remain unconvinced by the evidence. This is because, although ESP may exist, its practitioners to date have been unable to replicate their feats consistently and under strict laboratory conditions. Of course, many scientists assume because this is the case the so-called "psychic" is hoaxing.

The hallucination hypothesis is a deceptive category. While a few cases may fall into this area, surely most witnesses aren't hallucinating. And what about multiple witness reports? Mass hallucinations? It hardly seems likely.

This theory has taken a new twist in recent years with advocates of the "altered states" hypothesis. In short, it says that most Bigfoot sightings are vague and probably misperceptions. In a relaitvely few "hard core" close-up encounters, most occur to people who are alone, at night, in rural isolated areas; the same conditions under which people in laboratory settings have experienced vivid visions.

Now, you may think, "I've often been alone, at night, in isolated areas and never seen Bigfoot!" Under the vision theory, these environmental factors, coupled with a combination of internal conditions can trigger a dream-like experience. Internal conditions include: fatigue, emotional or physical stress, sleep deprivation, fasting, meditation or drug use.

Perhaps this can explain why witnesses appear to be sane, normal people, frequently passing polygraph exams, yet no absolute physical proof has been found.

If Bigfoot reports represent dream-like visions, why aren't encounters more varied beyond the general seven to eight-foot-tall, hairy, ape-like being? Why aren't descriptions around the world more reflective of the cultural beliefs of what Bigfoot should look like and how it should act? The answer is—they are. Creature descriptions are different depending on what part of the world you study. For instance, the Abominable Snowman or Yeti of the Himalayas is typified as having long, shaggy hair. The Chinese 'wild man' on the other hand is a bit shorter in stature, with a flatter face and red wavy hair.[10]

This same argument can be reversed to refute the vision theory. Believers in a flesh and blood creature will say that biological adaptations to different climates and geological conditions are part of the natural evolution of all living things. For example, animals living in very cold climates develop thicker layers of fur than their more southerly counterparts.

Australian paranormal researchers, Keith Basterfield and Mark Moravec are major proponents of the "altered states" or vision hypothesis. Sound far-out? Then consider the next case. Although the exception and definitely not the rule in Bigfoot encounters, such reports are not unheard of. From the early 1960s to July 1974, several reports of UFOs and Bigfoot occurred in the Yakima, Washington area. A young man left a group of friends to meditate alone near a stream. During this meditative state, he claimed to receive communication from a Bigfoot.

> A hypnotist regressed the percipient to the time of his first encounter involving amnesia of 1¾ hours. He related seeing something big visible from the middle up to the top and which put a hand on his shoulder. The creature (later described as dark brown with friendly eyes and unmoving mouth) communicated with his mind that he wanted help to get away from hunters, that he had a leader, and that he was willing to share fruit. The percipient saw a bunch of creatures looking down on him and he was mentally told that they were here before we were and that we are ruining their planet. The percipient declined any subsequent hypnotic regression sessions because it was 'too much of a hassle.'[11]

During ancient times there are scores of references citing the belief that fasting, sleep deprivation, while fatiguing the body while in dark or isolated environments, was thought to create magical experiences, such as enabling one to see a god or spirit. It appears that visions created during altered consciousness do play a role in Bigfoot reports. The unanswered question is, "To what extent?" While most Bigfoot reports occur in remote areas at night, of the cases investigated in this book, a substantial number involve multiple witnesses. Whereas typical characteristics of altered states are bright lights and the perceived speeding up and slowing down of time and/or amnesia on behalf of the witness, none of the cases in

New York and Vermont exhibit these characteristics. Hallucinations also do not leave footprints that sometimes go on for miles in very remote areas.

Our next category is Bigfoot as a prehistoric human, or a species so far unknown to science. Many people have trouble accepting the paranormal theories, which is why the "ape-man" hypothesis is still the most popular.

Dr. Warren Cook, Professor of Historical Anthropology at Castleton State College in Vermont, believes the evidence points toward a flesh and blood being, perhaps a hominoid.[12] He believes that creatures observed in the northeastern United States may be surviving relatives of a man-like being that once walked the continent of Africa about a half-million years ago; *Australopithecus*.

Cook's research indicates the creature possesses a keen sense of smell, a high intelligence, and a strong knowledge of its territory. These factors coupled with its apparent nocturnal behavior, physical strength and flexibility can account for the sightings, even though no absolute proof has been found. Cook says the descriptions and behavior patterns of the creatures sighted in the New York and Vermont accounts are "consistent with evolution, fossil finds and hominoid records."[13]

Other anthropologists, although in the definite minority, agree with Cook. Dr. Grover Krantz of Washington State University thinks the creature exists, and is more anthropoid than human. But even those who subscribe to the "ape-man" theory can't agree as to whether it should be classified as a highly evolved ape or primitive human. At a recent conference of the International Society of Cryptozoology (the study of unproven animals), Krantz advocated killing a Bigfoot so that scientists can study a dead specimen, an idea which horrifies those believers such as Cook, who feel Bigfoot, which appears to be shy and friendly, should be left alone.[14]

Another plus for a flesh and blood Bigfoot is history. There are numerous examples of species unknown to science until only recently. Writer John Keel provides a typical example—the first white man to see a gorilla in Africa:

> Scientists had a good laugh in 1856, when Paul du Chaillu returned from the Congo and described his en-

counter with a hairy giant. 'He stood about a dozen yards from us, and was a sight I think I shall never forget,' Du Chaillu reported. 'Nearly six feet high, with immense body, huge chest, and great muscular arms, with fiercely glaring large deep gray eyes . . . he stood there and beat his breast with his huge fist till it resounded like and immense bass drum.'[15]

History books are filled with similar examples of once thought to be mythical creatures which turned out to exist. On December 22, 1938, startled fishermen off the coast of South Africa, pulled up a coelacanth, a fish believed extinct for sixty to seventy million years.[16] And, on November 15, 1976, A United States naval research vessel discovered a previously unknown species of shark weighing 1,653 pounds.[17] Scientists named it *Magachasma pelagios*.

Despite widespread popularity of the nuts and bolts of Bigfoot theory—that it's some type of relative to modern man, there are many unanswered questions. Jerome Clark and Loren Coleman sum up these nagging drawbacks:

> . . . why, if they are real, are there no bodies, no bones, no live specimens locked securely in zoos and laboratories? Why only certain kinds of physical evidence, invariably of a somewhat ambiguous nature—footprints, strands of hair or fur, possible feces samples, and not others? The 'evidence' we have is always just enough to keep us from rejecting the reports as delusions but never enough to prove conclusively that unknown animals exist in our midst.[18]

Finally, we come to our last theory—that it's a phenomenon which is incomprehensible given our present evolution of science, comparable to a cat trying to understand Einstein's theory of relativity. This category could also be known as "your guess is as good as mine theory," or "anything goes."

If Bigfoot is part of the zoological rather than the paranormal world, then researchers and those concerned with conservation should take steps to ensure its protection. If such creatures exist, the scientific refusal to accept the existence of an animal without dissecting its corpse on a table is unfortunate.

If, on the other hand, Bigfoot is what researchers Loren Coleman calls a "creature of the outer edge of reality," then we're dealing with a different kettle of fish altogether. We may not have the answer to this riddle soon, but as Shakespeare once said, "There are stranger things in Heaven and Earth, Horatio, than are dreamt of in your philosophy."

References:

1. Moravec, Mark, *The UFO-Anthropoid Catalogue*, published by the Australian Centre for UFO Studies, 1980, p. 30, citing Worley, Donald, "The UFO-related anthropoids—an important new opportunity for investigator-researchers with courage." In Dombos, N.(ed.) *Proceedings of the 1976 Center for UFO Studies Conference*, Northfield, Illinois: Center for UFO Studies, 1976, pp. 291-292. A paranormal psychology and folklore expert, Moravec has compiled the largest known list to date; 72 documented summaries of Bigfoot-like creature encounters observed in conjunction with, prior to or just after UFO sightings in the same general vicinity of the creature observation. He lives in Pymble, New South Wales, Australia.
2. Moravec, Mark, *The UFO-Anthropoid Catalogue*, 1980, p. 23, quoting report by Leonard Stringfield cited in *Canadian UFO Report*, Vol. 3, no. 4, 1975, pp. 5-6.
3. Moravec, Mark, *The UFO-Anthropoid Catalogue*, 1980, p. 28, citing *Canadian UFO Report*, Vol. 3, No. 5, 1975, p. 1.
4. Moravec, Mark, *The UFO-Anthropoid Catalogue*, 1980, p. 16, citing Stringfield, Leonard, *Situation Red: The UFO Siege*. London: Sphere, 1978, pp. 79-80.
5. Moravec, Mark, *The UFO-Anthropoid Catalogue*, 1980, pp. 25-26, citing Stringfield, Leonard, *Situation Red: The UFO Siege*. London: Sphere, 1978, p. 77; Slate, B.A., and Berry A., *Bigfoot*. New York: Bantam, 1976 pp. 118-119; Green, John, *Sasquatch: The Apes Among Us*. Victoria, British Columbia; Cheam Publishing, 1978, p. 260.
6. Johnson, D.M., "The Phantom Anesthetist of Matoon: A Field Study of Mass Hysteria," *The Journal of Abnormal and Social Psychology*. April 1945, pp. 175-186.
7. Clark, Jerome and Coleman, Loren, *The Unidentified: Notes Toward Solving the UFO Mystery*. New York: Warner, 1975, p. 245.
8. Moravec, Mark, *The UFO-Anthropoid Catalogue*, 1980, p. 21, citing Clark, Jerome, and Coleman, Loren, *The Unidentified*. New York: Warner, 1975, pp. 22-23.
9. Ibid., pp. 22-23.

10. *New York Times*, January 5, 1980. Also, personal correspondence between Paul Bartholomew and Mr. Zhou Guoxing, anthropologist at the Beijing Museum of Natural History. Also see, Yuan Zhenxin and Huang Wanpo (with Fan Jingquan and Zhou Xinyan), *Wild Man: China's Yeti*. Fortean Times Occasional Paper No. 1. Published in 1981 by The Fortean Times.

11. Movavec, Mark, *The UFO-Anthropoid Catalogue*, 1980, pp. 26-28.

12. Personal interview with Dr. Cook by Bob Bartholomew, November, 1985.

13. Phone conversation between Dr. Cook and Bob Bartholomew, March 3, 1987.

14. Bord, Janet and Colin, *The Evidence for Bigfoot and other Man-beasts*. Whistable, Kent, England: Aquarian Press, 1984.

15. Keel, John A., *Strange Creatures from Time and Space.* Greenwich, CT: Fawcett Publications, 1970, p. 10.

16. *The Living Coelacanth*, British Museum of Natural History, Leaflet No. 10, 1975. Also, Zarzynski, Joseph W., *Champ, Beyond the Legend*, New York: Bannister Publications, 1984.

17. Zarzynski, Joseph W., *Champ, Beyond the Legend*, New York: Bannister Publications, 1984, pp. 34-35.

18. Clark, Jerome, and Coleman, Loren, *Creatures of the Outer Edge*. New York: Warner, 1978, p. 22.

CAPSULE SUMMARY OF CASES

1. Native American History, NY and VT
Algonquin Indian legends of the "Windigo," a "giant cannibalistic man."

2. Iroquois Indians, Western and Northern NY
Many tales are recorded of encounters with Bigfoot-like creatures called "Stone Giants."

3. 1604, St. Lawrence River, NY
French explorer Samuel de Champlain sails the St. Lawrence and logs Micmac Indian belief in the existence of the "Gougou," a giant, hairy human-like beast.

4. 1759, Northern VT
During French and Indian War, Major Robert Rogers and his band of rangers reportedly encountered "a large black bear" that often harassed them by throwing objects. The Indians called the creature "Wejuk or Wet Skine."

5. About 1770, VT towns of Morgan, Maidstone, Lemington, and Victory
Early settlers of northern Vermont report numerous encounters with large bear-like creature walking on two legs, nicknamed "Slippry Skin."

6. August 30, 1818, Sackett's Harbor, NY
Man observes hairy "wild man" emerge from woods, approach within a few rods, then flee.

7. About August 13, 1838, Silver Lake, PA on NY border (day)
Sixteen-year-old male shoots at small, boy-like animal that ducked behind a tree and fled.

8. Mid-October 1879, near Williamston, VT
Two hunters see five-foot man-like creature covered with bright red hair, having a long beard and wild eyes. One of the men fired, apparently wounding it. The beast charged the pair, they dropped their guns and ran.

9. **About November 22, 1893, near Rockaway, LI, NY (morning)**
Large "wild man" having "bloodshot eyes, long, flowing matted hair" seen on shore of Rockaway Inlet by "Red" McDowell and George Farrell while rowing boat.

10. **About November 23, 1893, Rockaway, LI, NY (evening)**
John Louth observes large hairy "wild man" by trees in Rockaway Park.

11. **About November 24, 1893, Rockaway, LI, NY (day)**
Susie Louth struck on back by wild man that springs from behind in brush, knocks her down, then runs off.

12. **November 24, 1893, Rockaway, LI, NY (early AM)**
Plumber William Tweedle attacked by "wild man" that threw him to the ground while hunting. It was eating a raw chicken.

13. **November 24, 1893, Rockaway, LI, NY (early AM)**
"Ned" Tracy shouts at large hairy "wild man" eating raw clams near shore.

14. **November 24, 1893, Rockaway, LI, NY (afternoon)**
House mover John Corning and assistant William McVay were working on beach when "wild man" attacked them.

15. **November 24, 1893, Rockaway, LI, NY (evening)**
Police chief McArthur's wife is seized from behind and choked by a "creature" which was scared off by Fred Sauer.

16. **July 26, 1895, Margaretville, NY**
Farmer William Cook attacked by a naked "wild man" about seven feet tall with big teeth after shooting at it.

17. **1890s, Moriah, NY**
William Napier tells of hearing boyhood stories of a Bigfoot-like creature spotted in area.

18. **February 1909, towns of Patchogue, Quogue, Eastport, Westhampton, NY (night)**
Residents of several Long Island communities report seeing a "baboon" or "monkey-like" creature on several occasions giving off a "blood-curdling shriek."

19. **Early November, 1922, near Babylon, NY (night)**
Armed police and civilian patrols search this Long Island community after sightings of a baboon or gorilla.

20. **1920s, near Schroon Lake, NY**
Strange bear walking upright seen by couple with surname of 'Wright.'

21. June 1931, Mineola, NY
Big ape-like hairy creature frightens several people near a Long Island nursery.

22. July 18, 1931, Huntington, NY
Sighting of a gorilla-like creature crashing through shrubbery recorded by a nurseryman and family. Police find tracks.

23. July 1931, near Huntington, NY
A farmer reports seeing a "strange animal" not far from the July 18 sighting in Huntington. Tracks found.

24. Early 1930s, Amityville, NY
An eight-foot-tall "gorilla with glowing red eyes" spotted on several occasions.

25. February 1932, Hamilton Co. near Blue Mountain Lake, NY
Famous Adirondack "wild man" sightings. A posse later tracked, shot and killed the "creature" which proved to be a Negro hermit in thick layers of animal skins.

26. August 25, 1934, North Massapequa, NY
Several reports of an unusual creature roaming this area of Nassau County, about five miles from Amityville. It is described as either a "man, beast or demon." A theory that it's an escaped chimp from nearby Farmingdale, LI is discredited by police.

27. September 4, 1934, Amityville, NY (night)
"Mysterious Apelike" creature tears up a garage. Concern builds to feverish pitch. During the night "most of the male residents of the neighborhood are sitting on their porches waiting for the animal with shotguns."

28. Around 1950, Greene County, NY (day)
Philip Winegard observed "monkey-like" creature about the size of a boy which "rose up out of the swamp and grabbed a bird in its hands."

29. 1951, Sudbury, VT
John Rowell and a Mr. Kennedy place 450-pound oil drum on tractor seat. The next day they find it several hundred feet away near Sudbury Swamp and 20" x 8" footprints leading from tractor to drum.

30. Early 1950s, near Rouses Point, NY
Family camping reports Bigfoot-like creature crossing road.

31. 1959, Whitehall, NY
Farmer Harry Diekel's neighbor tells of seeing bear-like creature on two legs.

32. **About 1960, Lewiston, NY**
Reports of Bigfoot-type creatures begin circulating in western NY.

33. **1961 or 1962, Plainfield, VT (night)**
Farmer William Lyford hears his cows making a ruckus. Investigating, he sees large, hairy creature with upright posture run off after pointing flashlight at it.

34. **Mid-1960s, Stockbridge, Rutland County, VT (7:30 PM)**
John Rose and several companions riding in pick-up truck see a seven to eight-foot grayish creature striding briskly across road on two legs.

35. **1965-1966, Sherman, NY**
White swamp monsters standing twelve to eighteen feet tall with six to eight-foot-long hair reported by family on several occasions.

36. **1966-1969, Mount Misery, Huntington, LI, NY (night)**
Several stories of couples parked in wooded Mount Misery area being terrified by a seven-foot-tall human-like monster.

37. **Fall 1967, near Ithaca, NY**
Reports of big, hairy Bigfoot-like figure in the woods during a major UFO wave in region. One report tells of a creature tearing a boy's jacket.

38. **January 12, 1969, Mt. Misery, Huntington, LI, NY (8 AM)**
Barbara LaMonica, J.P. Para and Richard DiMartino saw black figure of "something that resembled a human disfigured face" with "long black hair" in what appeared to be a "long black garment" retreat into bushes.

39. **Mid- March, 1974, Barre, VT (10 PM)**
Two men stopped along Country Club Road and tell Professor Warren Cook that they heard a "shriek" and saw "a tall dark figure running across a field . . . with hands that swung below the knees as it ran."

40. **July 1974, near Rutland, VT (after midnight)**
Eight to ten-foot hairy Bigfoot seen in vicinity and reported to police.

41. **December 7, 1974, Richmondtown, NY, (4:15 PM)**
Two young boys frightened by a big black "furry thing" while playing behind St. Andrew's Episcopal Church parking lot.

42. **January 21, 1975, Richmondtown, NY (10:45 PM)**
Nurse driving on Richmond Road observes black hairy figure cross road on two legs. Ten-inch, four-toed tracks found nearby.

43. 1975, Watertown, NY
Five-foot creature "swinging its arms" seen by Steve Rich, Jerry Emerson and another boy "just walking" on State Street Hill.

44. May 1975, Whitehall, NY (11:30 PM)
Skeene Valley Country Club owner Clifford Sparks encounters eight-foot-tall "great big" hairy "sloth-like" creature run off near first green of his golf course.

45. Late August/early September 1975, near Highgate Springs, NY
A man, his son and brother, observe a long-legged, wide-shouldered creature walking upright "at a casual pace" across a tractor trail.

46. Fall 1975, Whitehall, NY (night)
Whitehall Police Sgt. Wilfred Gosselin and brother, Russell, hear eerie high-pitched yell lasting over a minute while hunting at intersection of Abair Road and Rt 22A.

47. June 1975, near Saranac Lake, NY (night)
Two men see "Bigfoot" squatting by Rt. 3. They stop and approach, but it walks away.

48. June 1976, near Watertown, NY
Two boys claim to see eight-foot Bigfoot covered with black hair. Fifteen-inch tracks found in vicinity.

49. August 11, 1976, near Watertown, NY
Two teenage boys see hulking, black, hairy creature in woods.

50. August 24, 1976, Whitehall, NY (night)
Martin Paddock, Paul Gosselin, Bart Kinney report seven to eight-foot brown, hairy creature in field off Abair Road. Whitehall Police Sgt. Wilfred Gosselin checks area and sees "an awful tall shadow."

51. August 25, 1976, Whitehall, NY
Farmer Harry Diekel finds "big human footprints" in field near intersection of Abair Road and Rt. 22A.

52. August 25, 1976, Whitehall, NY (midnight)
Whitehall Police Officer Brian Gosselin and anonymous NY State Trooper saw a large, two-legged creature off Abair Road, coming to within thirty feet of Gosselin's car. The seven to eight-foot creature had "big red eyes that bulged about half an inch off its face, no ears, no tail, dark brown hair, almost black; the arms swung down past his knees." After about a minute, the trooper shone a light in its eyes and it ran off screaming.

53. **August 26, 1976, Hampton, NY**
Anonymous Whitehall High School official observes a large hairy, ape-like creature walk up out of Bixby's Apple Orchard and cross in front of his car.

54. **About August 26, 1976, Whitehall, NY**
Sheriff's deputy and trooper find and make plaster cast of nineteen-inch footprints near Poultney River Bridge, East Bay area.

55. **About August 30, 1976, Whitehall, NY**
Trooper watches large, furry figure seventy-five to one hundred yards off in Abair Road field.

56. **September 1, 1976, Whitehall, NY (11:10 PM)**
Nearby Granville resident tells Whitehall Police, "I shot Bigfoot" in field off Carver's Falls Road. He and others claim ten to twelve shots fired.

57. **September 7, 1976, Whitehall, NY**
Trooper finds several 19½-inch human-like tracks by Poultney River near Abair Road.

58. **September 1976, Lewiston, NY**
Police Officer Peter Filicetti and mother report Bigfoot-like encounter in cornfield. Unusual footprints found.

59. **Fall 1976, Oxbow, NY (night)**
Raccoon hunter sees seven-foot hairy creature walking on two legs.

60. **October 1976, Chittenden, VT**
Prominent Rutland, VT area businessman wishing anonymity, takes photo on nature trail in northeastern Rutland County. When developed, the picture shows possible huge Bigfoot-like creature.

61. **Late 1976/early 1977, North Central VT**
Two people driving along road startled by two Bigfoot creatures running next to car, pacing it.

62. **March 1977, Whitehall, NY (day)**
Royal Bennett and granddaughter Shannon observe "stump" in field off Fish Hill Road. Suddenly, the "stump" stood up and a honey-colored creature, seven to eight feet tall, estimated at 500 pounds walked off. Large human-like track (13½ inches) found in vicinity that spring by Bill Brann.

63. **March 1977, Chittenden, VT**
Housewife glances out window of house and sees ape-like creature standing in field. Its shoulders are slouched with arms hanging at its sides, staring toward horizon. Husband comes with gun, but creature already gone.

64. July 1977, Northwestern Saratoga County, NY
Family finds fourteen by six-inch footprints while camping near Big Eddy.

65. July or August 1977, Clarendon, VT (night)
James and Nancy Ingalls see man-like creature while driving home from roller-skating. Its eyes glowed red in headlights. Next day, fourteen to sixteen-inch prints like naked human feet found.

66. 1977, near Theresa, NY
Two separate sightings of a large, hairy creature by two pairs of railroad workers. Prints found at both sites.

67. Early August 1978, Whitehall, NY (night)
Man and dog terrified by "inhuman" screams outside his house on Abair Road. Dog acts strangely.

68. September 1978, Porter, NY
Hunters find carcass of large, partially decomposed ape-like animal in field near Lewiston, NY. Carcass lost, but experts believe pictures of body are of a black bear.

69. November 28, 1978, Shrewsbury, VT
David Fretz family startled by fourteen to sixteen-inch human-like tracks (four inches deep) in snow around their house.

70. Late November 1978, Morrisville and Craftsbury, VT
Fantastic stories of a Bigfoot-type creature dubbed "Goonyak" circulate across area. It allegedly killed farmer's bull. Probable hoax.

71. December 1978, Kinderhook, NY (dawn)
Mrs. Martha Hallenbeck observes "big, black, hairy thing all curled up" on her lawn.

72. About May 17, 1979, Whitehall, NY (7:30 PM)
A Fair Haven man, his mother, father and sister-in-law saw a hairy, man-like head peering over bushes. After the man yells at it, it runs off with inhuman gait. About a week later, he and the same group of relatives experience similar incident, again while fishing on East Bay River.

74. December 6, 1979, Kinderhook, NY (day)
Barry Knight watches four great big furry things on two legs crossing a creek while trapping on Cushing's Hill.

75. 1979, Whitehall, NY
Mr. "B" and friend observe large creature with big stride walk "over" a fence.

76. Late 1970s, near Saratoga Lake, NY (night)
Sheriff's deputy investigates reports of loud screams at trailer park. He finds ten-inch-diameter tree ripped from ground and thrown against trailer.

77. April 1980, Kinderhook, NY (day)
"Barbara" sees 7½-foot creature with reddish brown fur in cornfield while driving on Rt. 9. It looks "like a highly evolved ape."

78. June 1980, near Lawrenceburg, NY (3:30 AM)
Fred Ranaudo encounters Bigfoot "breathing real hard, like it had asthma," while camping. Fifteen-inch prints found.

79. September 24, 1980, Kinderhook, NY (11:22 PM)
Several members of the Hallenbeck family, including Martha, Barry Knight, Barbara Knight, her daughter, Chari, and granddaughter, Melanie, are terrorized by Bigfoot-like beast outside Martha's home. Shots fired.

80. November 1980, Kinderhook, NY (night)
Barry Knight and Russell Zbierski heard screams while walking remote road near Cushing's Hill. Suddenly, five hulking figures with cone-shaped heads converged in the road ahead of them. A third (female) witness just down the road watched Bigfoot take food from garbage at about the same time.

81. Winter 1981, Adirondack Park Region, Northeastern NY
Cross-country skier finds footprints with unusually long strides.

82. Winter 1981, Bullhead Mountain, near Indian Lake, NY
Hunter follows eighteen-inch human-like footprints for one mile, leading to ledge. Unusual cone-shaped hut found in vicinity.

83. February 1981, near Kinderhook, NY
Ten-inch, three-toed footprints found in snow-covered field resembling enormous duck tracks. Bruce Hallenbeck taped them on movie film. Tracks mysteriously end in middle of field.

84. April 1981, Kinderhook, NY
A woman bicycling on Novak Road is startled by a big hairy thing lumbering across road and into cornfield.

85. May 8, 1981, Kinderhook, NY (night)
Several campers, including Barry Knight, observe tall figure walking on two legs with long arms and no neck, in vicinity of Cushing's Hill. One of them sees two glowing red eyes high off the ground.

86. June 1981, Kinderhook, NY
Strange three-toed tracks, fourteen inches long, seven inches wide, found.

87. Summer 1981, Catskill Mountains, Columbia County (night)
Several reports of Bigfoot-type creatures, including one from a chemist, his wife and two children who report multiple encounters with a black, hairy beast or beasts. They found sixteen-inch tracks. Family lived about twenty minutes from Kinderhook.

88. September 8, 1981, Kinderhook, NY
Rabbit hunter finds huge human-like prints by Kline Kill Creek.

89. November 1981, Kinderhook, NY
Woman spots "big two-legged thing, reddish-brown, which then ran off into woods."

90. 1981, Davenport, NY
Two children fishing encounter Bigfoot-like creature that gives off a bad smell and screams.

91. Early February 1982, Whitehall, NY
Two law enforcement officers see a hairy Bigfoot creature cross Rt. 22 near Washington Co. Highway Department garage by South Bay.

92. Spring 1982, Austerlitz, NY (day)
Hunter startled by eight-foot, red-haired Bigfoot.

93. May 5, 1982, Kinderhook, NY (10 PM)
Bruce Hallenbeck hears very loud noises like chattering monkeys. Suddenly, a strange white ball of light rises into sky and vanishes with a sound "like a balloon popping."

94. May 1982, Kinderhook, NY (late PM)
Michael Maab is fishing near dam and sees eight-foot, reddish-brown Bigfoot creature apparently observing him twenty yards away. It has beady eyes and black fingernails. After two minute staring contest, it ambles into woods.

95. Summer 1982, Kinderhook, NY (dusk)
Bruce Hallenbeck's father sees large, black hairy creature "standing out under a big tree in the yard."

96. September/October 1982, near Kinderhook, NY
Several reports of a "white Bigfoot" in area.

97. December 1982, Chatham, NY
Several unverified reports of a white Bigfoot creature in Chatham, near Kinderhook.

98. March 1983, Tinmouth/Pawlet, VT
While traveling rural road, Connecticut couple inform Prof. Cook that they encountered a "giant of a 'man'" that walked along a rocky ledge. At one point, the creature raised his "giant arms above his head and waved them several times" in a frantic display.

99. **About August 1, 1983, Dexter, NY**
Seven-foot creature seen by resident near hardware store.

100. **September 1983, Kinderhook, NY (9 AM)**
Large black bear-like animal walks in front of elderly gentleman's car on Novak Road.

101. **October 7, 1983, Moose Mountain Pond, near Indian Lake, NY (night)**
Richard Newman and son, Eric, hear loud crunches while fishing. Eric spots two large hairy legs passing by.

102. **October 7, 1983, Town of Lake George, NY (7:45 PM)**
Three young men are cycling four miles south of Lake George Village on bike trail. They cycle off after hearing screams and seeing big red eyes seven feet off the ground in woods.

103. **Winter 1983, Whitehall, NY (day)**
William "Bud" Manell finds strange footprints in snow by Whitehall dump in East Bay region. The tracks have very long strides.

104. **1983, Eagle Bridge, NY, near Stephentowne**
A large unidentified creature spotted.

105. **February 1984, Kinderhook, NY**
Two hunters near Cushing's Hill find enormous tracks in snow and bloodless rabbit carcass nearby.

106. **April 1984, Windsor County, VT (5:30 PM)**
James Guyette was driving north on US 91, within sight of Hartland Dam. He saw huge, hairy "animal-man come up the bank near the brook, walking fast down the road at an angle" one hundred yards away. It was "tall and lanky with arms swinging" and "head shaped like a helmet attached to a uniform in the back."

107. **May 6, 1984, near Kinderhook, NY**
Large human-like tracks—the biggest 13¾ inches found by bridge.

108. **May/June 1984, Washington Co., Whitehall & Hartford, NY (dark)**
Series of bizarre laughing screams heard in several locations.

109. **Spring 1984, Chittenden, VT (night)**
Man told Ted Pratt he heard a loud scream and something ripped his cellar door off (solid two-inch oak), then prowled in basement. Possible track found but destroyed.

110. **June 1984, Hubbardton, Rutland County, VT (3:30 AM)**
Bruce Bateau heard shrieking-whistling noise while in bed. Next day, he and mother, Mrs. Barnard Bateau, found large naked footprints with three distinguishable toes. Musty/musky smell.

111. 1984, Essex and Caledonia Counties, VT
Man sees huge, hairy ape-like creature at edge of open field in northwest corner of town. Tells Audrey Beam he wishes to remain anonymous.

112. 1984, Clarendon, Rutland County, VT (early AM)
Couple claims to see large, hairy ape-like creature near junction of Rt. 7 and Rt. 103, south of Rutland. Vermont State Police do not appear to take report seriously.

113. 1984, Hubbardton, VT
Anonymous man "J" tells friend he saw hairy creature in the northwestern corner of town.

114. August 20, 1984, Whitehall, NY
Seven to eight-foot creature on two legs seen by residents.

115. August 28, 1984, near Whitehall, NY
Seven to eight-foot creature on two legs. Approximately 400 pounds.

116. March 4, 1985, North Clarendon, VT
Mrs. Dorothy Mason and son, Jeffrey, found 16" x 5" tracks in snow around their new home.

117. March 1985, Whitehall, NY
Woman finds large tracks in snow in yard on 4th Avenue. Human-like prints come from nearby tree-line and circle her home.

118. May 4, 1985, Castleton, Rutland County, VT (9:50 PM)
Young-sounding female phones Prof. Cook and refuses to give name. Claims to have just seen seven-foot creature, covered with hair outside her house. She sounds sincere, but suddenly connection is broken. Possible hoax.

119. June 16, 1985, Kinderhook, NY (11:05 PM)
Mrs. Margaret Mayer is startled while driving on Rt. 203 by six to seven-foot bizarre creature with yellow eyes, appearing something like a cross between a bird and Bigfoot. Creature is covered with light-colored fur or feathers.

120. June 1985, Peacham, Caledonia County, VT (evening)
Two fishermen in boat on Foster Pond see hairy form on shore (possibly two). Bear-like creatures on two legs striding like a man—then breaking into a run. Fishermen came near shore to get a better view. Feet are lighter-colored than rest of body.

121. July 6, 1985, Kinderhook, NY (8 PM)
Martha Hallenbeck sees round, white "eyes"—two sets—seven and five feet off the ground near her porch. After ten to fifteen minutes they disappear. "I've never seen anything so bright white."

122. September 20, 1985, West Rutland, VT (7:30 PM)
Al and Bob Davis, Frank "Fron" Grabowski III, Roscoe Jones are involved in Bigfoot incident two miles west of West Rutland near Ed and Theresa Davis' home. Entire family hears strange noises. Bob and Fron see "gorilla-like" creature standing upright, approach them. After tossing stones at it, in reaction to the being originally throwing stones, creature retreats. Bob notices peculiar black skin under eyes. Jones also sees it. Next day large footprints found by Fron and cast by Dr. Cook.

123. September 20, 1985, West Rutland, VT (8 PM)
Susan Cook (Prof. Cook's daughter) sees a Bigfoot while driving on Rt. 4A, some two miles west of West Rutland.

124. October 1985, Proctor, Rutland County, VT
Burton "Burt" McCullough Sr.'s chicken coops at his farm on West Proctor Road ripped open, fence torn, numerous chickens killed. Several huge human-like tracks dot area around coops.

125. November 20, 1985, Chittenden, VT (6:30 PM)
Two young boys playing near house when one turns to see Bigfoot creature thirty-five feet off. He empties BB-gun into it, then flees into house.

126. November 21, 1985, Chittenden, VT (8 AM)
Rickie Siefert and Corey St. Lawrence are on school bus turning around opposite Mt. Top Inn. Spotted big, black, hairy creature crossing field. He and Corey say it wasn't a bear.

127. October 1, 1986, West Rutland, VT (8 PM)
Castleton College students John Brandt, Kerry Bilda and George Dietrich almost hit nearly seven-foot-tall Bigfoot while driving on Rt. 4A about two miles west of West Rutland. Its body had collie-length hair but its white face was virtually hairless. The incident happened within 300 feet of Susan Cook's encounter of September 20, 1985.

128. October 26, 1986, Poultney, VT (9 PM)
Jill Cortwright and Kathy Quill sight a long-haired Bigfoot crouching on the side of Rt. 30 between Castleton Corners and Poultney. Cortwright confident "it was no bear."

129. 1986, Norton Pond, Northern VT
A Bigfoot-type creature seen by a professor from Vermont's Johnson State College, as described to Wes and Olga Gordeuk of Cromwell, CT. Later, large tracks were found in the area.

130. February 11, 1987, East Poultney, VT
Two Castleton College students cross-country skiing, find large barefoot tracks in the snow.

131. October 9, 1988, Kinderhook, NY (2 AM)
Susan Hallenbeck, a teacher at Ichabod Crane Middle School, heard strange sounds like gorillas made in the movie, "Gorillas in the Mist."

132. August 1989, near Poestenkill, NY (11:30 PM)
An Averill Park couple encounters a "large, upright figure . . . tall and reddish-blond in color and running very quickly."

133. August 18, 1989, Hampton, NY (3 PM)
Sixteen-year-old boy sees a seven-foot-tall, one-yard wide creature which peeked at him while he walked along Rt. 22A South.

134. August 24, 1989, Hampton, NY (2 AM)
Two camping teens observe six-foot creature with "glowing red eyes" circle their campsite.

135. August 28, 1989, Hampton, NY (1 AM)
Two boys heard a "loud and . . . steady" vocalization which "continued for at least three minutes."

136. Mid-September 1989, Clemens, NY
A Clemens man hears strange screams and grunts while his dog begins reacting wildly to the presence of strong, offensive odor.

137. Mid-January 1990, Ghent, NY
Human-like tracks found in the snow measuring over twenty inches long. Days later, similar tracks are found in snow in same area, disappearing into a thicket.

138. July 1990, Whitehall, NY
A "tall, big, dark" figure is seen crossing a field off County Rt. 21.

139. March 1991, Loon Lake Mountain, Franklin County, NY
Herbert Francisco finds oversize human-like tracks, eighteen to twenty-two inches long with ten-foot strides.

140. Early April 1991, Long Lake, Hamilton County, NY
Katherine Kaifer reports sighting a Bigfoot creature.